Rev. Moss Ntlha has produce[ ] dealing with important quest[ ] [Chri]stianity and spirituality. Both Christians and non-Christians wrestling with the issue of African Traditional Religion will find that important matters are addressed in this amazing testimony of an African woman. This book covers a range of issues of relevance to Christian discipleship, ethics and public policy. To proclaim Christ as Lord in the context of religious pluralism and a post-apartheid sociocultural context is bound to be challenging. This book does it with commendable sensitivity.

Dr Elijah Maswanganyi
Founder and Director of Christ is the Answer Global Ministries

By writing the story of Francinah Baloyi, Moss has helped those involved in African Christian mission and discipleship to wrestle with deep issues affecting African spirituality. He is helping to bring clarity on a number of issues that for some may be contentious and affect the very core of who they are. Moss deals with matters deemed difficult by many in a clear and loving way. I highly recommend this book.

Peter Tarantal
Associate International Director of OM
Chair of the Global Leadership Council of WEA MC

This is an engaging, thought-provoking and challenging mirror of Christianity and personal journeys in Africa. It may be equally so in many other parts of the world. There are many issues that do not easily find their way onto the table of Christian conversations due to the uneasiness that they bring. This leaves many individual Christians, particularly African Christians, having to wrestle alone with difficult matters that affect them directly – a lonely and painful journey. The story of the character in this book illustrates this point so well. Joseph Galgalo writes, "Christianity has received impressive reception but still lives as a stranger within the African home." Brother Moss Ntlha is consistent in asking difficult questions that are often left unasked. These questions lead to helpful and transforming conversations. I commend this book to all – both those who are serious about the journey of faith and those who are still not sure and have not started. It demonstrates in a powerful way God's presence in all areas of our existence in and outside of the church. Let the conversation continue and inspire all of us to ask the questions towards a more meaningful following of the Lord Jesus Christ.

Rev. Ziphozihle D. Siwa
President of the South African Council of Churches
Presiding Bishop of the Methodist Church of Southern Africa

Once I started reading this book, I could not stop! *Out of the Shadows of African Traditional Religion* is a powerful testimony concerning the conversion of a young South African woman who was steeped in the traditional religion of her people. God stepped into her life of sin, waywardness, rebellion and abortions and radically transformed her through a vision of Jesus, heaven and hell. She repented of how she had lived before, destroyed all that belonged to the old ways as a sangoma, and set about the task he had assigned her. This true story vividly brings to mind Paul's experience on the road to Damascus (Acts 9). 2 Corinthians 5:17 rings true: "Therefore, if anyone is in Christ, he is a new creation. The old has passed away; behold, the new has come."

Francinah's story demonstrates that conversion must affect every aspect of our life and challenges the syncretism that is threatening the church in Africa. This book is a must read for all African believers, teachers and students of African Traditional Religion, missionaries, and pastors.

Samuel Waje Kunhiyop
General Secretary of ECWA
Author of African Christian Ethics *and*
African Christian Theology

OUT OF THE SHADOWS OF AFRICAN TRADITIONAL RELIGION

OUT OF THE SHADOWS OF AFRICAN TRADITIONAL RELIGION

CHRIST'S DELIVERANCE OF A SANGOMA

Moss Ntlha

CONTENTS

ACKNOWLEDGEMENTS

Writing this book has been a wonderful journey for me before writing, during writing, and after the last word was written. Months passed from the time I first heard about Francinah's story and felt the inner promptings to write it. Initially, I wanted to find someone else to take on the project, but in the end it fell to me. When I finally reconciled myself to the task, the Lord connected me with wonderful companions to help in the journey. Anneke Rabe, my good friend and a wonderful intercessor, offered to pray along with me throughout the months of writing. The ministry colleagues, friends and church leaders who encouraged me are too numerous to mention them all by name, but I will make special mention of Johannes Malherbe and Rocky Ralebipi, who went through the manuscript and offered helpful feedback and encouragement. I also thank my friend and mission colleague Johan Theron of HRT who encouraged the project from the beginning.

Special mention must be made of the help I received from Langham Partnership and especially from Isobel Stevenson and her amazing team who read and reread the manuscript and provided most helpful editorial advice to guide me through the entire process.

Special gratitude must go to my wonderful wife and partner in faith and ministry, Khumo, without whom the book would never have happened. She introduced me to Francinah Baloyi and her incredible testimony and provided invaluable feedback and support along the way. Along with my daughter Masereko and son Kutlwano, now newly married to his beautiful wife Mamotlhabane, she endured endless hours of writing and interviews. I am ever so thankful for this family.

Finally, I am grateful to the Lord Jesus Christ who chose to show Francinah all that he did, and that in a small way I can contribute to the cause by telling the story.

I should be greatly honoured if some pilgrims in the faith find encouragement in the pages of this book. More so if some would find the clarity they need to feel able to bow the knee to Christ as Lord.

PREFACE

Christians from every continent and every culture owe it to their Lord and Saviour to tell their story as a testimony of what Jesus has done for them. In this way, the power and integrity of the gospel will be available to people everywhere as a testimony to the uniqueness of Christ and his readiness to save all who call upon his name. Their stories will also reveal what it means to have a contextualized faith, which is an essential element in authentic worship.

It is my hope that Francinah's story will be of help to fellow Christ-followers in Africa who are looking to bring the gospel "home" to Africa. They are in good company with the African eunuch who, intrigued by the story of the God of Israel, took the long journey to Jerusalem to worship him (Acts 8:26–39). Returning home to Africa, he was mulling over the theological questions the gospel in the Book of Isaiah posed for him. There must have been as many questions then as there are now. The God of heaven always has his eye on those who earnestly seek him, keen to answer their questions. He sent Philip along to assist the African in his Bible reading, and Philip answered his questions to the point that the eunuch felt ready to commit. The same God reached out to Francinah in her need.

Francinah's story also raises and answers African questions about God, redemption, and the spirit world. While it is an African story, it is also relevant to those who are not African, for the theme of human redemption and deliverance from spiritual bondage is a universal one.

This book is a result of many interviews with Francinah, and with people close to her, including family members, friends and church colleagues, all of whom attest to the truthfulness of her testimony.

1

UNUSUAL ENCOUNTERS

The year was 1988, and the day was Monday, the 1st of August. At 10:00 a.m. on that windy morning she booked herself into Kalafong Hospital, near the black township of Atteridgeville. Her pain was unbearable, and she was bleeding. Her medical records show that she, Francinah Baloyi, was in for a dilation and curettage procedure. A medical routine all too familiar to township women who found themselves in the unhappy and lonely place of taking the life of their own unborn child under the harsh and cruel conditions of backstreet abortions.

Beyond the physical pain she had endured since Friday when she aborted, Francinah was emotionally and spiritually drained. She had learned early in life to be tough and take responsibility, but with four abortions weighing on her soul, she had little inner strength left. If she appeared strong, it was because that was easier than admitting this was killing her inside.

Since Friday Francinah hadn't eaten anything, and she was not feeling hungry. She had no appetite. All she wanted was to feel better again, to reclaim her body, and her life.

The reason she chose Kalafong, rather than Ga-Rankuwa Hospital near her home, was that the nurses in Ga-Rankuwa would know her, and most likely offer her an unsolicited sermon about the dangers of backstreet abortions. After all, she had been there only a year earlier following her third abortion. For a sum of R100, one could have a backstreet abortion. Some enterprising nurses had seen an opportunity to make a quick buck from desperate women who wished to terminate a pregnancy. All perfectly illegal, of course.

But what were poor women to do in apartheid South Africa? They were too poor to travel to other countries where abortion was legal and could be done in the safety of a good medical facility. That option was only open to their more well-heeled sisters.

Francinah was twenty-three years old, trying to eke out a living in the sprawling urban township of Ga-Rankuwa, far from her grandparents' homestead in the village of Taolome. She worked as a cleaner at a caravan park that was owned and administered by the municipality of Pretoria, but that was not her only job. She was also a sangoma whom people paid for help when they were in trouble.

Francinah struggled alone with the moral anguish of choosing to end the life of her unborn child. The memory of the deep poverty in which she was raised, into which her siblings would no doubt slide if she did not support them, was a compelling factor in her decision to abort. Though unwed, she also already had two children. She could see the dark clouds of poverty beginning to gather around her.

She always made sure that she acted quickly, as soon she knew she was pregnant. She reasoned that if she could terminate before the foetus was fully formed, it would not be too bad. After all, before then, human life had not really begun. In her view, abortion was only wrong if the human form had already taken shape in the womb.

The South Africa of 1988 was blighted by apartheid. This soul-destroying, dehumanising socio-political system caused great harm to the mind, body, and soul of African people. The United Nations condemned its social engineering as a "crime against humanity".

Yet apartheid had its redeeming features. Among those was the legal protection it offered to the unborn. Out of character with its generally wicked logic, it recognized that human life – black or white, even in its foetal stage – bears the image of its Creator. For that reason, life must be cherished and protected. Therefore, abortion was illegal in apartheid South Africa, a legacy of the Calvinistic heritage of those who crafted the apartheid state. Of course, once the baby was born and its blackness confirmed, other laws kicked in that conspired to damn it from cradle to the grave. The only place where black life was safe was either in the womb or in the grave. Everywhere else, it was a hazardous affair.

The First Two Abortions

The stories of Francinah's abortions are tragic and worth telling. Beyond the menace of looming poverty that she was sure would catch up with her if she did not make a plan, there were other factors at play that led to her falling pregnant and then having to abort.

As a rural girl looking to fit into the urban life she had chosen when she came to live on the outskirts of Pretoria, Francinah felt under pressure from friends and her social circle. To be different and live by her village values would mark her as the odd one out. She soon met and fell in love with Joseph. As their relationship developed, she looked forward to one day being his wife and bearing his children. They would live happily ever after. In spite of her traditional upbringing, no one had ever told her that sex with someone you are not married to is wrong. Besides, almost everyone she knew was doing it. It didn't take long before she fell pregnant. She had never thought she would have to deal with pregnancy until after marriage.

Then there was the matter of the clash of cultures that got in the way of the normal methods of preventing an unwanted pregnancy. Francinah could easily have gone on the pill. Contraceptive pills were freely dispensed at medical facilities in the township or in Marabastad near her workplace. She knew all about prevention. She even attended family planning sessions at the local clinic and accepted pills from them. But she never used them.

The reason was that the world of *badimo* – the world of her African ancestors who were revered as intermediaries between the living and the Creator God – is different from the Western world with its culture and medical science. Badimo have their own ways of dealing with medical problems, and Western medicine was not one of them. More particularly, the pill was not one of them. Francinah was a sangoma and practised African traditional medicine. African traditional healers have an aversion to the ways of Western culture and medicine. They have their own means, their own diagnoses, and their own prescriptions. So Francinah used those faithfully.

She was baffled when she kept falling pregnant. Why, she wondered, were the gods lining up all these children for her when she did not want them, while so many other people were struggling to conceive?

Her first daughter, Kedibone, was born in 1978. Francinah was eighteen years old at the time, and she decided that one child was all she would have and be able to take care of. Her boyfriend was not supportive, and Francinah found herself alone, struggling to feed and clothe her child. This made her more determined not to have another baby.

A year later, in 1979, she conceived again. She was not prepared for the pregnancy, so she started talking to friends about abortion. They organized a concoction for her, mixed in what looked like dirty water, and assured her that it would take care of the problem. It looked terrible, and Francinah felt she could not bear to look at it and drink it. So she figured she would go to sleep and wake up in the early hours of the morning, while it was still dark. That way, she would not have to see what she was drinking!

But, around midnight she had a dream. The message in the dream was that the concoction was dangerous and would harm her. Thankful to her ancestors who were watching over her, she woke up and spilled out the concoction. In this way, her son Winston's life was spared. He was born on the 9th June 1979.

Reluctantly, she reconciled herself to being the mother of two children, but was determined that there would be no more. She would do all she could to ensure that her children escaped the poverty she had endured.

Unfortunately, she fell pregnant again in 1980. Taking counsel from friends who knew these things, her mind was quickly made up to terminate the pregnancy before it went too far. If she acted quickly, she was given to believe, the blob of tissue in her womb could be taken out before it became a fully formed human being. Backstreet abortion was the only option she had. Francinah had her first abortion that year. It was relatively problem free. There were no physical complications, although the psychological anguish lingered. She did not have to go to hospital to seek treatment for any after-effects of the abortion. She told herself that the baby had not yet formed. A return to the rhythm of daily life helped her put it all behind her. She was able to move on with her life.

In 1982, she fell pregnant again. Again she determined to have an abortion since she knew from experience that she could expect no support from her boyfriend. Although he held down a good job, Joseph was unhelpful financially. So she kept the news about the pregnancy from him and confided instead in a friend named Ouma, explaining to her why she was intent on termination. Ouma counselled against it, but Francinah's mind was made up.

Ouma decided that the only way to save the baby was to let Joseph in on the secret of the pregnancy. So one day while visiting Francinah and Joseph, Ouma noticed a heavily pregnant cat passing nearby. She seized the moment: "Francinah, look at that cat! It's like you!"

That got Joseph's attention. "What do you mean Ouma?"

"Yes, Francinah is pregnant, like that cat. And she wants to abort the baby because she feels that you are not really supportive."

Joseph was both excited and disturbed: excited that he was going to be a father again, but disturbed that his baby could be aborted. He pleaded with Francinah, assuring her that he would be supportive in raising the child. Francinah believed him and brought the baby to term. That was how Susan was born. Sadly, true to his ways, Joseph was not helpful at all. He only once bought milk for the baby.

In 1984, another tragedy struck! Another unwanted pregnancy, raising the same dilemmas as the previous one. To keep the baby was to invite poverty into her home and introduce her children to suffering and avoidable economic hardship. So Francinah made a plan and terminated the pregnancy. But this time she suffered complications and lost a lot of blood. An ambulance was called to pick her up from her workplace and take her to nearby Kalafong Hospital in Atteridgeville, where she was admitted in severe pain.

To say that she was scared is to understate the terror that gripped her soul. She did not know what to expect and how long she was going to be in hospital.

When Francinah overheard a nurse remarking, "She has lost a lot of blood," she froze.

It could only mean one thing: She was going to die!

Fear descended upon her, enveloping her like a dark cloud. Francinah started to weep, thinking about her children and what would happen to them when she was no longer around to look after them. She imagined them struggling, eating from dustbins, with no one to help them. She broke down.

She was still weeping when she was carried to the ward on a stretcher just after two in the afternoon.

A Strange Dream

Francinah must have cried herself to sleep, because she found herself having a strange but reassuring dream.

In her dream, she saw the ceiling split open, allowing the entrance of a person clad in white. Though it was a dream, it had a sense of reality that touched her soul. As a sangoma, Francinah was alive to the world of the spirits, but she knew that this person was different from the spirits she was accustomed to. As he descended towards her, she became aware of his tremendous love and compassion.

"Why are you crying, Francinah?" the man asked.

"My Lord," she heard herself say, "I am crying because I am going to die, and my three children will have no one to raise them. They are going to suffer like I suffered when I was growing up."

The person responded with love and assurance, "Do not be afraid; you will not die. You will return to your home and see your children again." Then he disappeared.

Francinah awoke, mystified by the dream, but feeling reassured that she would make it through the operation that awaited her. She felt deeply thankful for the dream and was able to relax in the confidence that she would not die. She turned to other patients in the ward, flashing a genuine smile as she greeted them. She hadn't noticed them when she was brought into the ward earlier that afternoon, overcome with sorrow.

A little while later, her name was called repeatedly on the intercom: "Francinah Baloyi, 19h00 theatre ... Francinah Baloyi, 19h00 to theatre!" Her moment had come.

Once again the fear of death welled up within her, sweeping away the assurance her dream had brought her.

She started to pray, promising God that she would never again have an abortion.

A few women who were awaiting the same operation were milling about as though in a support group of their own. Francinah shared her anguish with them.

"Don't worry, Francinah, you will come out alive," they said. "We have also had abortions, and here we are! Alive and well."

Francinah could feel her heart sink. "Maybe you just had a miscarriage and that is why you survived. As for me, the abortion I did was deliberate. God will not forgive me and will not allow me to be resuscitated after the operation. He will simply take my soul!"

Just then a rather careless nurse said something about the possibility of dying and not making it through the operation. It was difficult to tell whether she was trying to discourage the women from having backstreet abortions or whether she was merely stating the facts as she knew them. In a cavalier and unprofessional way, she told all those lined up for the operation, "All of you who pray to God must pray now. You don't know if you will come back from theatre alive. If you pray to the ancestors, go ahead and do so. If you want snuff to help you communicate with your ancestors, we will arrange it for you. If you use muti (a concoction often prescribed by sangomas to avert bad luck or witchcraft), use it. Pray to whatever gods you are comfortable with, because this might be your last day on earth. Several people have already died today, and the hospital mortuary is already full! We won't have space for you, so we will have to just throw you on the mortuary floor!"

Francinah's heart sank even lower. *This nurse is most definitely referring to me*, she thought to herself.

She started to weep. Her heart was pounding. Another nurse had to leave everything and take her aside, "Francinah why are you so afraid? Why is your heart rate so high?"

Francinah took the nurse into her confidence and confessed her fears.

After a while they managed to calm her down sufficiently to be ready for the operation.

Thankfully, she made it through alive. True to her reassuring dream, she was back home after an overnight stay at the hospital.

The Third and Fourth Abortions

Once back home, it was business as usual. Francinah's prayer and promise to God fell by the wayside. By 1987, she had another unwanted pregnancy. A third abortion was done. This time, she went to Ga-Rankuwa Hospital for clean-up care after the abortion.

Francinah's friend and confidant, Elizabeth Botjie, recalls the events of Friday, 29th July 1988, when she gave her friend, who was pregnant again, a piece of her mind about her choices. As they left work for the weekend that day, she told Francinah, "Do not go for an abortion. It is very dangerous, and you could die."

"Ok," replied Francinah as she made her way to her home. It was an unconvincing response, and Elizabeth suspected that Francinah had not made up her mind to do the right thing.

"If you abort, you must never talk to me again," Elizabeth threatened as she made her way to board the bus home. She felt it was time to draw the line on Francinah's careless ways. She had had enough.

Later that evening, Elizabeth was relaxing in her home, unwinding from the week's hard work, hoping against hope that her friend would do the right thing. There was a knock at the door. It was Francinah, looking sickly.

"What's wrong?" Elizabeth enquired, trying to make eye contact as she opened the door for her. Francinah avoided her, looking down. The word *guilty* was written all over her face.

"*Eish, hape nna ke tlhoo ira abortion.*" (I have done the abortion.)

Francinah looked like she had been through a rough time. She could have gone to spend the weekend with her family as she usually did, for her children stayed with her mother on weekdays when she was at work. But her aunt was strict and would probably not tolerate what she had done. Neither would her mother, who lived in Winterveldt. She too was very strict and would probably have thrown her out. Not so Elizabeth.

Elizabeth's motherly instincts kicked in. She forgot about the line she had drawn in the sand. Her friend was in pain, and this was no time for interrogations. She welcomed her into her home and started to nurse her, making her comfortable. Francinah needed someone like Elizabeth to be by her side for the weekend. She had no one else she could confide in who would love her unconditionally and overlook her repeated iniquities.

Elizabeth offered her food to eat, but Francinah could not eat. The only thing she felt able to ingest was her favourite drink, Sprite, and some hot water.

Later, as Francinah's pain grew worse, Elizabeth started to arrange for a neighbour who had a car to be on stand-by just in case she needed to go to hospital during the night.

"Should I take you to Ga-Rankuwa Hospital?" Elizabeth asked.

"No," Francinah groaned defiantly, though quite obviously in pain. "I don't want to go to Ga-Rankuwa. Those nurses will remember that I was there only last year for the same reason. I will persevere until Monday, then I will go to work so that an ambulance can be called to take me to Kalafong," she offered. Elizabeth was unconvinced, but she knew better than to try to persuade her headstrong friend. So she went along with the warped logic that could very easily have ended Francinah's life.

They made it through the Friday night, and with great difficulty through Saturday and Sunday.

In great pain, assisted by Elizabeth, Francinah made her way to the bus stop on Monday morning, taking the usual route to the municipality where they worked. Upon arrival, Elizabeth duly reported Francinah as sick and needing an ambulance. So after her backstreet abortion on the 29th July, Francinah was in hospital again on Monday, 1st August 1988. This was the fourth time she had gone down the road of ending the life of an unborn child, and the third time doing so put her in hospital. She was becoming a "hardened criminal", ignoring even the warnings of her ancestral guardian spirits. Each time she aborted, she faced the very real danger of septicaemia and dying of complications resulting from the abortion.

Francinah hadn't been back to Kalafong Hospital since her abortion in 1984. Besides, there would be no cost to her to travel there. She timed the abortion so that she would arrive at work sick on Monday morning, and an ambulance would be called in to rush her to Kalafong. If all went well, she would be in and out and back at work by Tuesday, ready to get on with her life.

Francinah's assumption that she would slip in and out of Kalafong under cover of anonymity was a big miscalculation. As she went through the admission procedures, a nurse recognized her. "You are Francinah Baloyi, from Ga-Rankuwa township? I know you. You have come for yet another abortion complication?" Her cover was blown. Remarkably, the nurse remembered her from her 1984 visit to the hospital. This was strange, because thousands of patients went through Kalafong Hospital each week!

Francinah is strong, quick-witted, and humorous. Knowing that the best form of defence is attack, she fired back, "I have not come to a police charge office. I have come to a hospital to be nursed and assisted." She was putting on a hard exterior to hide the pain she bore inside.

Eventually Francinah was sent to the ward, where she would await her turn to go to the operating theatre. It was to be a long wait, from 10 o'clock in the morning till evening. There was enough time for a thorough soul searching, which was prompted by a strange but firm "word" that dropped into her mind and spirit. "This time you have gone too far; you will not make it through the operation. You will die."

It was the third time Francinah had this premonition. The first time was when her friend Elizabeth Botjie heard of her plans to abort and warned her that it could be a fatal mistake. Elizabeth was an older woman who welcomed Francinah to the municipality where they both worked and became a close friend. The two had a bond of love, loyalty and friendship. Francinah confided in Elizabeth when she was ready to start her journey as a sangoma. When Francinah finished her initiation as a sangoma, Elizabeth was with her at her final welcoming ceremony. But through all the earlier abortions, Francinah had consistently ignored Elizabeth's counsel, downplaying the seriousness of what she was doing and determined to go ahead with the abortion.

The second premonition had come earlier that morning, around 4:00 a.m. The ancestor spirits had made their displeasure known regarding Francinah's serial abortions. And now this third premonition, this "word" whose origin and source she was uncertain, was occupying her mind. Was it from God? Was it from the ancestors? She did not know for sure.

Before Francinah came to hospital, she had begun to prepare herself to meet her Maker. True to traditional African belief, she knew there is a

God who is Sovereign and the Creator of all things. Her ancestors were intermediaries to God. She reckoned that God would take a dim view of her series of abortions.

So in the days leading up to her abortion, Francinah started taking seriously the brief prayer and devotional that came up just before the seven o'clock news on the state-owned South African Broadcasting Corporation. It was the policy of the apartheid national broadcaster to "preach" the Christian message. That was one of the ways the Christian faith earned the dubious honour of giving the apartheid state a veneer of legitimacy. Not surprisingly, no one else in Francinah's family bothered to watch this devotional. They followed African traditional religion and would take the appearance of the cleric on the screen as a signal to leave the room. In those days, there were no other channels to watch. Francinah decided to stay in the room to learn more about Christianity. She reasoned that, when she eventually appeared before God after her death, the fact that she had listened to the preacher on the TV would count in her favour. God would see that she was not as bad as the other members of her family.

Francinah recalled how, at the time of her second abortion in 1984, she had promised God that if he spared her life, she would change her ways. She had not kept her part of the deal. She knew that if God took her life now, he would be perfectly justified. She had gone too far. So she concluded, *Whatever would be would be. God would have to judge.* She was resigned to the idea of dying and finally meeting her Maker if the operation was to end her life.

An Unusual Visitor

The clock on the wall read 7:00 p.m. when Francinah was finally wheeled out to theatre. She noted the time because she hadn't eaten all day, partly because she hadn't felt like eating since Friday, but also because she had been told that she would not be fed until after the operation. Sometime later she was wheeled back into the ward, operation completed. She was thankful to have made it through alive.

But Francinah couldn't sleep. Her anaesthetic was wearing off, and she was in pain. It was nothing compared to the excruciating pain she had when she arrived at the hospital on that Monday morning, but it was still bad. She sat up on her bed, shivering as if in the grip of a cold winter. Was it because of the operation, or were her sangoma spirits announcing their arrival? Were they expressing their displeasure at her being in a white man's hospital?

Soon Francinah could feel a spirit "coming up" from deep within her soul, wearing her body like a garment and bidding her to chant the traditional *ngoma*.

Francinah was embarrassed and tried to suppress the spirit of Koko, her paternal grandmother, long since deceased and yet living in her. Koko was one of seven spirits that accompanied and enabled Francinah in her work as a sangoma.

Francinah recalled that at around 4:00 a.m. that Monday morning, before she got ready to go to work and on to hospital, Koko had woken her up, angry at her for the abortions she had done. Koko had rebuked Francinah for her misdemeanours and for going against the values of *ubuntu* – the African value system that holds that human life is to be cherished, whether that life is of the departed, of the living, or of the yet to be born. Ubuntu requires that you treat others as you would like to be treated, for each person is someone in community with others.

So Koko's displeasure was directed at Francinah for having yet another abortion. That is why, Koko had explained, Francinah's ancestral spirits were not intervening in the many things that were going wrong in her life.

As she sat up on her hospital bed, Francinah bowed her head as if to whisper to Koko to please not come now but wait for her to get home from the hospital. Koko was having none of it! She had arrived, and Francinah had to join in Koko's chanting of the traditional sangoma song.

Just then, Francinah sensed a strange presence in the room. Lifting her head slightly to look, she saw a strange light. Slowly her head rose, tracing the light. Where her feet were supposed to be, she saw just light – intense, gentle and beautiful. It was different from the light in the room, or any light she had ever seen. The upper body of the presence, though discernible, was covered with this heavenly light. Francinah knew instinctively that it was Jesus, the same person who had reassured her before her previous operation.

Francinah was not a Christian. She was a third-generation sangoma. Six of her ancestors were sangomas. Both her parents were sangomas. Her upbringing did not include church, at least not in any sense that suggested commitment. What hymns she knew were those she had picked up at social gatherings, funerals, weddings, or from school. Nothing in her upbringing and young adult life had prepared her for what was happening.

Jesus did not say a word. In silence, he stretched his hand towards her, as if pointing deep inside her soul. His finger seemed to take hold of Koko within her. Like a magnet, it dragged Koko out of her body and smashed her on the floor. Francinah saw Koko disappear into thin air in front of her! She was confused! Why was this man doing this to Koko?

He pointed to her again. Francinah could feel the second spirit that possessed her, Ntatemogolo, coming up from deep within. She tried to warn him not to come because this stranger had just chased Koko away! She feared the same fate would befall Ntatemogolo. But Ntatemogolo insisted he was with Koko, and where Koko went, he went.

Ntatemogolo was similarly dispatched. Four other spirits came up and met the same fate.

Finally, the last spirit came up. This was the most powerful one, the one Francinah relied on for help with the most difficult cases she encountered as a sangoma. She was a water spirit, and Francinah had gone to the river for her initiation into a covenant with her. This spirit, human from the waist up and snake-like from the waist down, sat on her lap, shaking and making murmuring sounds like Francinah herself used to make when she was under the spirit's control. Its dreadlocked hair covered its face, and it seemed as if a contest of powers was underway. Francinah looked up to see what was going to happen. She thought that this last spirit would put up a fight and chase the stranger away, so that her ancestors could return to her. Alas, the same fate befell the water spirit. Jesus made the same movement with his hand, pointing to her. As if drawn by a powerful magnet, the spirit came out and was smashed to the floor, where it disappeared as had all the others.

Francinah had been a sangoma for six years. While her spirits were with her, she had felt strong and able to do her sangoma duties: healing the sick, countering spells and curses, protecting people from witchcraft, helping people win court cases, curing bad luck, and providing numerous other services to her clients. Now her guardian spirits were gone! She could no longer claim to be a sangoma. She felt robbed and alone, yet strangely, she also felt a sense of freedom.

For a brief moment, Jesus stood at the foot of the bed, without saying a word. Following the clash of powers, in which the ancestral spirits were methodically and ever-so-effortlessly routed, Francinah sank back on her bed, not knowing what to think, or how to think. Many thoughts rushed through her mind. What had just happened to her? She had no language to describe it. Who had ever heard of ancestral spirits, the powers upon which generations of her family line had relied, being dealt with in so disrespectful a manner? How would she explain what had just happened to her mother, her family, and her people? Was she dreaming, or was it all real?

It was quite clear that she could no longer claim to be a sangoma. Her spirit guides were no longer with her. A superior power had cast them out. She was left alone. Part of her wanted the ancestral spirits back. After all, they were her gods. They gave her a sense of comfort, power and belonging, as well as a sense of her place in the universe. Without them, Francinah felt somewhat alienated from herself. But part of her was curious about the meaning of it all. Would it last? Was she finally free from the spirits that she had tried to run away from in her earlier years?

Her wonderings were interrupted by Jesus approaching her and moving closer to where she lay.

2

THE EARLY YEARS

Bakensberg is one of several chiefdoms that have survived in the area that is today called Mokopane, just two hours north of Pretoria, along the N1 freeway. These chiefdoms, namely Kekana (Moshate), Langa (Mapela), Lebelo (Grasvlei), and Langa (Bakensberg) represent the migrations of various peoples – Tsonga, Shangaan, and Ndebele – who criss-crossed the Southern African region in the last three hundred years and eventually settled there.

The Ndebele of Chief Langa, in whose village of Bakensberg Francinah was born, are the result of the migration of Zulus/Hlubis from the clan of Langalibalele. They travelled north from the Mahlabathini area near modern day Pietermaritzburg in the 1690s.

As a Tsonga-Shangaan, Francinah's roots were traceable further east to Mozambique, where the Tsongas are known to have lived as early as the sixteenth century.[1] In the 1820s, their relatively peaceful existence was interrupted by the invasion of the warrior and general Soshangana, who fled from Shaka during the Mfecane wars. Finding fertile land in Mozambique, Soshangana settled there after conquering the smaller, peace-loving tribes who were living in the area, including the Tsongas and founded the Shangaan kingdom in Mozambique.[2] Some of those

---

[1] J. D. Kriel and J. B. Hartman, *Khindlimukani Vatsonga: The Cultural Heritage and Development of the Shangana-Tsonga* (Pretoria: Promedia, 1991), 16.

[2] Kriel and Hartman note that "between 1838 and 1840, various Tsonga groups, fearing subjugation by Soshangana, fled westwards from Mozambique over the Lebombo Mountains into South Africa. The most important groups of Tsonga fugitives were the Nkuna, Valoyi, Mavunda, and Hlave, who settled mainly in the north of the present Gazankulu." *Khindlimukani Vatsonga*, 17.

whose lives were disrupted by these events moved into the uninhabited areas of the Lowveld or settled in the northern and north-eastern Transvaal as subjects of the Venda and Sotho tribal chiefs.[3]

It is conceivable that Francinah's family name evolved from Valoyi to Baloyi after interaction with Ndebeles and Sothos in the Limpopo/Mokopane area.

Like most South African rural towns, Mokopane has deep marks of history etched upon its collective soul. If you peeled it like an onion, you would find layer upon layer of African traditionalism, ethnic differentiation and tribal wars, European colonialism, apartheid, African resistance to the twin evils of colonialism and apartheid, and more recently, a transition to a post-apartheid social order. All of these layers continue to mark the life of the town to this day. The different names by which the town has been known over the last two hundred years, namely Vredenburg, Potgietersrus and now Mokopane, bear testimony to this reality. It is a town in search of identity. It mirrors a similar identity crisis experienced by post-apartheid South Africa as a whole: a nation trying to reinvent itself after the many skirmishes in its troubled past; a nation reaffirming its gods and resisting any colonial imposition across cultural, religious, economic, and political fronts.

As the warm summer of 1960 was coming to an end in Bakensberg, Agnes and Samuel Mthombeni were preparing themselves to welcome their firstborn, Francinah. She arrived on the 4th February. She was followed in time by her two younger siblings, brothers Phineas and Caiphus.

Following the collapse of the turbulent and abusive marriage of their parents, the three children were joined later by their half-sister Selina and half-brother Andries, both born to Agnes out of wedlock.

The family was steeped in African traditional beliefs. In the pre-1994 South Africa where Francinah grew up, these beliefs were mainly below the surface of the nation's spiritual landscape. Christianity was the hegemonic religion of the time, with other faiths relegated to their own cocoons, barred from enjoying their fair place under the South African sun. Public spaces, like schools, prisons, hospitals, parliament and other public institutions were "Christian" spaces. Proponents of

---

[3] Ibid.

African traditional religion say that the fact that it survived for millennia without being codified in text is testimony to its resilience against heavy odds. It endured because it is a lived religion, written in the dreams and lives of African people. It is not possible to fully understand African cultures without taking account of their religion.

The sidelining of African traditional religion was to change with the overthrow of the system of apartheid. Freedom meant, among other things, a reclamation of pre-colonial and pre-apartheid African religious identity.

African tribes and families, like tribes and families elsewhere, have a distinct religious and cultural worldview. They believe in the transcendent Other and hold to a particular way of finding meaning and redemption with the Other. This religious belief manifests differently from tribe to tribe, and even from family to family. Liyong comments on this worldview:

> As far as we are concerned, everybody has his shrine guardian, every family has a shrine, every clan or tribe has its major shrine and array of gods and goddesses. It is inconceivable to imagine a person or group without religion. The religion of your clan belongs to you. You never go from clan to clan selling, hawking your god, young, old or mythical. When guests come, European or Arab, you welcome them in your name, the names of your ancestors, on behalf of their ancestors.[4]

The sangoma cult was an important way in which Francinah, like most Africans who espouse this basic tenet of African traditional religion, understood how the living communicate with the ancestors, and how the ancestors in turn mediate on behalf of the living to God (who is spoken of as *Modimo* in the Tswana/Sotho language group).

Both Francinah's maternal and paternal grandparents were sangomas.[5] They were devout in the practice of African traditional religion, as were Francinah's biological parents.

---

[4] Taban Lo Liyong, *Culture is rutan* (Nairobi: Longman, 1991), 120.

[5] Different African tribes use different names for their traditional healers or diviners. Tswanas, Sothos, and Pedis use *ngaka*, Zulus use *sangoma*, and Shangaans refer to their healers as *n'anga* or *mungoma*. For most tribes in South Africa, "sangoma" is used colloquially to refer to a traditional spiritual healer.

Growing up in her parents' home, Francinah knew all about the *gandelo*, or altar where the family could communicate with the ancestors. As a child, she would kneel by this altar and watch the elders in the family do this. Traditional rituals and blood sacrifices, which were made annually or more regularly according to the need, were also typical of the way the Mthombeni household practised their religion.

At birth, Francinah was named Makhanani Mthombeni after her maternal grandmother, Makhanani Baloyi. She stayed with her parents until she was nine years old, when conditions at home deteriorated so badly that she had to relocate to her maternal grandparents' homestead in Taolome, about ten kilometres away.

Francinah's father, like most people, had a bright and a dark side to him. On the bright side, Francinah and her siblings experienced him as a very protective man who would never let anyone harm them. He never lifted his hand to beat them except one time, recalls Francinah, when he beat her with a *lefielo* (an African broom).

Mum and Dad had left earlier that day to go work in the fields. There was no food to eat in the house; not even the usual left-over porridge. Since Francinah, at seven years of age, was the oldest of the children, she had to find something to give her little brother. So she mixed together a concoction of flour, sugar, and maize meal stirred up in cold water and fed it to him. Because it was sweet, he ate a significant helping. But several hours later, he developed bad constipation and began to struggle to breathe. His tummy started to swell. Francinah started to panic.

Fortunately for her, the weather changed. Thick clouds gathered, and soon a torrential rain began pelting down, making it impossible for the parents to continue working in the fields. So they hurried back home and found the little boy in a perilous condition.

"What happened? What did you do to him?" Samuel demanded, concerned that if he did not know what Francinah had fed the child, he could not help him. Francinah was frightened, but she refused to answer. Samuel called for help from the neighbours, who were able to get the boy to vomit. Thankfully, this was enough to stabilize his condition. Eyes darting around the little mud hut, Samuel looked for what Francinah could have fed the boy. He soon found the offending mug containing what was left of the concoction she had fed him.

That was the only time Samuel Mthombeni lifted a hand to mete out punishment to his daughter.

Francinah has fond memories of how he was supportive in all her cultural rites of passage. When she was ten, she had to go to *komeng*, a traditional initiation school where the girls attending ranged from eight-year-olds to twenty-year-olds (the latter had often come from the city, and had not grown up in the village). That was where Francinah was given the name Ramasela, replacing the name Makhanani. Though she is Shangaan, she went to the Basotho ba Leboa initiation because that was the dominant tribe in the area.

Five years later, when she was fifteen years of age, Francinah went to a Shangaan initiation school, where she was again called by the Shangaan name of her paternal grandmother, Makhanani. At both of these initiation schools, as well as when Francinah became a sangoma, Samuel was present. As an African man, this was the most expressive way of showing his love and support for his daughter. He was always there to support her daughter, even when she no longer stayed with him. Some of the paraphernalia that Francinah received when she was inducted as a sangoma were gifts from her father, who was also a sangoma.

But Samuel also had a dark side. He was given to too much drinking and violent outbursts. Francinah's mother, Agnes, bore the brunt of his abuse, which frequently played out in full view of the children. At times when the abuse got to be too much, Agnes would fetch Francinah from school and flee from the village, along with her other two children. She would go and stay with friends for weeks, which affected Francinah's schooling.

Samuel never held down a job, and scarcely worked two months in a year. Even when he was working, it made hardly any difference to the family's circumstances. He seemed to work only long enough to get sufficient money to buy drink. The Mthombeni homestead consisted of two virtually bare mud huts. One was used as a kitchen, although it had none of the normal kitchen furniture one would expect to find in a hut. In fact, it had no furniture at all. That was where they made a fire to warm themselves when the temperatures plummeted or when the weather outside was unfavourable. The other hut was used for sleeping. It also had no furniture or beds such as one might expect to find in a bedroom. The children slept on the floor, using old fishing nets that had been used to fish in the nearby river as blankets.

If the Mthombeni household represented the typical shape of rural poverty, Agnes was its face – abused, poor, unemployed, female, and chiefly responsible for caring for three children and an abusive husband.

Like many rural women, Agnes was caught in a vicious circle of abuse and poverty. A veritable backbone of the family, she was hard-working and would go to great lengths to make sure there was food for the family to eat. She would ask neighbours for food, often in exchange for doing their washing. She would go from house to house, covering large distances in search of opportunities to exchange her labour for food. Anything would do – cleaning houses, making bricks, working the fields – anything, as long as she could come home with some food. Sometimes she would get eighty kilograms of maize meal as payment for a backbreaking toil. That would provide food for a month – or would have, if Samuel had not succumbed to the temptation to barter some of it in exchange for beer. His habit of doing this greatly frustrated the young Francinah and her mother, but they knew better than to try to get in the way of his addiction.

Agnes's efforts to scrape together enough food to keep the family alive were not always successful. On such days, the family would sleep hungry and hope she would be luckier the next day.

Even in the village, Christmas was an occasion when many people would splash out. There would be plenty of food and new clothes and toys for the children. But the poverty of the Mthombeni household was accentuated by the relative plenty and merriment of their neighbours. Rather than Christmas being the time of "good news to the poor" that it was meant to be when the Prince of Peace came into the world to "proclaim good news to the poor", it was often the worst time in the Mthombeni household. Francinah has a vivid memory of staying huddled in the hut with her siblings on Christmas Day with hardly any food to eat because her mum could not find anyone to whom she could sell her labour.

If there was one thing that Agnes and Samuel had in common, it was their protectiveness towards their children. But she was also a disciplinarian. She believed that sparing the rod would spoil the child, even though she would not allow anyone else to beat her children.

Francinah remembers once when Agnes fought with her brother – Francinah's uncle – for daring to punish her daughter for some misdemeanour. Agnes went berserk! She was unstoppable when she went on the warpath to defend her children. On that occasion, she ignored Grandpa Baloyi's attempts to stop her fighting with her brother. Exasperated, Grandpa picked up an axe and hit Agnes over the head!

Schooling

It was when Francinah started school at Thutlwane Primary in Bakensberg that her name changed from Makhanani Mthombeni to Francinah Baloyi. Many black South Africans found themselves having to get English or Christian names as a sign that they were civilized and educated. This was necessary in government and business institutions, presumably for the benefit of white South Africans who found it difficult to pronounce African names. When one factors in the missionary influence on the public policy of South Africa at the time, it is also possible that African names were ditched as heathen and uncivilized. Christian names were given to suggest that someone was now converted to the Christian religion. These names were also given in order to harmonize interactions between whites and blacks in the church, workplace and public institutions.

The name "Francinah" was more or less picked up on the street as Agnes was walking along, holding her daughter's hand, on the way to register her for her first year in school. Agnes was wondering what Christian name to give her. She thought aloud, as if to include Makhanani in her thought process. Could she name her Sophia? It was a good name, but there was a bad girl in the village called by that name. So she thought again. What about Francinah? That was the name of Agnes's sister. It seemed a nice name. So when Makhanani's turn came to sign in at Thutlwane Primary, she was registered as Francinah Baloyi.

The school was on a hill about an hour's walk away from Francinah's home. She would join other children from the village on the long walk there and back, for there was no school bus or any means of transport. The road went past a church in the village. Every day as she walked along the road to school, she would see a man clothed in white standing at the church. To her surprise, none of her schoolmates could see him. Along the stretch of road from the church to the school, she would sense that this person was walking along with her. She couldn't explain it to anyone, so she kept it to herself.

On Wednesday mornings the whole school would gather for prayer and worship. That was where Francinah learned some Christian hymns. *Moya o mokhetwa etla, o nkishe thereshong* [Come Holy Spirit and lead me to the truth] and *Nna ke rata ho sepela nao* [I want to walk with you, oh Lord] were her favourites.

While singing these songs, Francinah would look through the window and see the man in white clothes sitting on a rock just outside the school hall where the assembly was held. The man would be looking intently at her. Francinah would start crying, not able to explain to anyone what she saw. At that early age, she could not understand what was going on. She did not know that she was to meet that same man later in her life.

The Move to Taolome

Francinah was a bright child and did well in school, even though she had no academic support at home, since her parents were both illiterate, her father being worse off than her mother in that regard. Her mother could manage a little reading and writing, having been taught by her little sister who used to come home after school and teach her what she had learned for the day. It was from this little bit of learning that Agnes would on occasion assist her daughter Francinah with writing.

But the abusive relationship between Samuel and Agnes soon spilled over to the children and began to negatively affect them and their schooling. Eventually Francinah's maternal grandparents intervened and took her away from the Mthombeni household in order to give her a more stable environment. She had to change schools, leaving Thutlwane Primary and instead attending Claremont Bantu Primary, which was closer to her grandparents' home. If she and the other children left at 6:30 in the morning, they would be at school by 7:30 after an hour's walk. The Bakenberg high school, however, was a three-hour walk from her grandparents' homestead.

For her part, Francinah was relieved to leave the Mthobeni household at Bakensberg, even if it meant separating from her father. She felt that she was leaving behind a sad and dark chapter of her life. Beyond the emotional torment of watching the violent outbursts and drunken rage that her father directed at her mother, she had suffered much embarrassment among her school friends and classmates. This was especially so when her mum marched into the school to fetch her so they could escape the domestic abuse.

Life with her mother's side of the family promised to be more bearable and orderly. The Baloyis were much better off economically than the Mthombenis. By village standards, they were rather middle class. They owned livestock and had a big house with a corrugated iron roof, in contrast to the traditional mud hut with a thatched roof Francinah had lived in before. They ran a small shop from the family compound, selling groceries and other necessities to people in the village. Agnes and her children moved back there in 1970, and two years later, when Francinah was twelve, her parents divorced.

Francinah's expectation that life at the Baloyi's home would be easier was soon dashed. Her grandfather nursed a grudge against Agnes because she had disobeyed him and married Samuel Mthombeni, whom he regarded as a poverty-stricken loser with no business marrying into a prestigious family. He did not take well to the fact that his daughter had defied him. Not one of his other children had dared do so. Nevertheless, he welcomed her children into his home, which already accommodated his four wives, Agnes's siblings and a number of their children. Francinah found herself surrounded by many cousins, the children of her uncles and aunts.

While the grandparents were angry about Francinah's marriage to Samuel, they did not take it out on the children. It was the aunts who caused trouble. They were the ones who "managed the economy" of the Baloyi household, and they disliked the fact that Samuel's children were now their responsibility. So Francinah and her siblings paid the price for being Samuel's children and for Agnes's defiance of their father. While the other children in the household were given access to food, clothing and pocket money, Agnes's children were not. It didn't help that Francinah was always top of her class in school, while her cousins did poorly and even dropped out of school. Family jealousies only made matters worse.

When Francinah was thirteen she experienced the depth of her aunt's hatred of her and her mother. It was a day when her mother had been sent by her grandfather to buy some groceries in town. By then, Agnes had a nine-month-old child by another man. Francinah was left to babysit her nine-month-old half-brother.   At around 9 a.m. her aunts pressured her to feed the child some porridge. She ignored them initially, but they continued to insist that she must feed him, and so she did. But she was surprised to see that the baby seemed very weak and had porridge coming out of his nose – even though she had not yet started feeding him. She called out to her aunts for help, and then to her shock, the baby died in her arms!

The aunts did not appear particularly concerned. They simply took the baby's body and ordered her to wash his clothes. This ritual of washing the clothes of the deceased is normally done by adults, in preparation for a family ceremony when the clothes are passed on to members of the family who can use them. It is not a task normally assigned to a thirteen year old.

Tearfully Francinah started to wash the clothes. She was still in shock at her half-brother's dying in her arms and was consumed with guilt, feeling that she was somehow responsible for his death. She was terrified about what would happen when her mother returned. Knowing her mother's temper, Francinah was sure she would be killed for allowing the baby to die.

She was still busy with the washing when her mother came back. Agnes was surprised to see what Francinah was doing and asked where the baby was. The question cut into her like a razor blade. Consumed by guilt and fear, Francinah fled to the nearby hills. She could hear her mother's anguished wailing as the news was broken to her.

Francinah only dared to return when other relatives came to her and assured her that her mother was not angry with her. Agnes had thrown her sangoma bones and knew that it was witchcraft that had taken the life of her child.

It was after this incident that Agnes left to look for work in Pretoria. She never returned to the village, abandoning Francinah and her siblings with their grandparents. Naturally, things became worse for Francinah and her siblings, for previously Agnes had fought for them and defended them against abuse.

The family in which Francinah was growing up was very traditional. African cultural practices reigned, and the Christian religion was taboo. The children were not allowed to go to church at all. Any of them who accepted a friend's invitation to go to church would be punished by being denied food, clothes and toys. They were told that going to church was a sign of disloyalty to the ancestors, who were understood to be responsible for the family's ability to put food on the table. So Francinah knew almost nothing about Christianity beyond what she learned at school. Yet she was always top of her class in Bible studies, performing even better than children who were raised as Christians.

It is a testimony to her determination to get an education that while in high school, she often had to leave home at 2:00 a.m. to start the ten kilometre walk to be at school by 7:00 a.m. Often without pocket money or food to eat, she would start the long walk back home after school, arriving at eight in the evening, just in time to wash, eat what food there was, and sleep.

At first, Francinah had the comfort of walking the long distance with five or six other kids. But when a bus became available for the trip back from school, the other kids would get on the bus. Francinah had no money for the fare, and so she would walk back home alone through the bush as the darkness of dusk gradually enveloped her.

In spite of the lack of time to study due to the long walk, with hunger a constant companion, Francinah performed well at school. But sadly her schooling would eventually succumb to the harshness of the treatment she and her siblings endured.

The crucible of suffering often produces fine virtues in a person. So it was that this harsh upbringing gave Francinah an acute awareness of the suffering of others. Even as a child she would often burst into tears at the sight of suffering. She also developed a keen sense of justice and fairness and would come to the defence of those who were wronged. Even now years later, when she is leading a flourishing Christian ministry, she still remembers her formative experiences. Her brother Phineas recalls how she constantly reminds him never to forget where he comes from and to ensure that he is always there for his children.

3

THE CALLING OF THE SPIRITS

At the age of sixteen, Francinah's adolescent years were interrupted by the arrival of the spirits into her life. As she puts it in the vernacular, "*Ke ne ka tsenwa ke badimo*" (The ancestor spirits came to me).

The career of a sangoma can start in various ways. It can start through a sickness that Western medicine appears unable to tame or control. A diviner then discerns that the disease has spiritual roots and that the ancestors are calling on the patient to respond accordingly. Or the role of sangoma can be transmitted intergenerationally, so that the gifting is passed on from the departed to the living. Some people also seek to be become sangoma's because of the prestige a sangoma enjoys in a traditional community, and because they want the power to heal and work miracles, and gain wealth.

A 'sacred' dream is often the way that the ancestor spirits signal their intention to admit someone into their service as a healer or prophet. Dreams are thus regarded as a meeting place between the ancestors and the living, and the medium through which the departed communicate with the living. The living, in turn, communicate with the departed through invocations, rituals, and sacrifices or through the mediation of sangomas. This two-way communication channel is a well-established manner in which, in the African worldview, the living and the departed remain in communion.

So it was with Francinah.

One winter day in June 1976, during the school break, Francinah secretly left her grandparents' home in Taolome. Her mission was to look for her mother, who had never come home since she left for Pretoria. Francinah knew that her grandparents would not allow her to embark on the long and dangerous journey to the city alone. However, Francinah was so desperate to find her mother that she was not deterred. Until then she had never ventured outside the safe villages of Taolome and Bakensberg in Mokopane. She did not even have a forwarding address for her mother. She only knew that her mother lived in Ramogodi village near Ga-Rankuwa, where she stayed with her uncle.

Francinah's bravery can probably be attributed to the fact that a year earlier, when she was fifteen, she had endured the rigours of the Shangaan initiation school. For many African communities, the rite of passage from girlhood or boyhood to adulthood is mediated through traditional initiation schools. These schools instil virtues of discipline, courage, and bravery along with grounding initiates in their culture and value system.

Francinah stole one rand from her grandmother and got her uncle, who was working for the railway company, to buy her a ticket from Potgietersrus to Pretoria North. The money was only just enough for the long overnight trip. Dressed only in a t-shirt and a skirt, with a little bag containing a few clothes, Francinah set out on her journey.

For the warm weather of Mokopane, the clothes she wore were probably sufficient, particularly during the daytime. By night-time, however, the winter temperatures had dropped dramatically. Francinah was quite clearly underdressed for her journey. Hunger was another challenge, although that was the least of her worries. Her ability to go without food had been honed during the long walks to school and back.

It was just after midnight, when the train snaked into Pretoria North. Thankfully, Francinah had met a relative who was travelling on the same train, headed for Johannesburg. He told her to alight at the Pretoria North Station, assuring her she would have no problem finding her way.

Francinah got off the train and started to wander around in the dark, asking passers-by for directions. A nice Xhosa man came to her assistance. He spoke no Shangaan or Pedi, and Francinah spoke no Xhosa, and so they had to resort to using sign language in an attempt to communicate. Finally, in desperation, he signalled for Francinah to follow him to his workplace in Wonderboom, where a colleague was Shangaan-speaking. It was an hour's walk in the freezing winter night.

They reached his workplace at around 2:00 a.m. There he reported to his boss that he had picked up this lost girl in the streets, and asked if anyone could assist her. His colleague, a Mr Maluleke, spoke Shangaan and could easily communicate with Francinah. The boss helpfully allowed him to leave early in order to help point Francinah in the right direct to find her mother. He would take the train home and ensure that when he disembarked at Taylor's Loop, he would leave her in the care of the ticket examiners there.

Francinah and Mr Maluleke went back to the train station and boarded the train to Taylor's Loop. By the time she disembarked, it was 4:00 a.m. The area was known to be dangerous by night, but much better in the daytime. So Mr Maluleke gave her strict orders to wait at the station until the sun was well up, which would be around 9:00 a.m., before she ventured onward in her journey to find her mother.

By ten o'clock that morning, another Good Samaritan pointed Francinah in the right direction, and she found the little shack that Agnes called home. She was renting this accommodation on someone's property.

Francinah knocked at her door.

"Come in" came the answer. Relief filled Francinah's heart as she heard her mother's voice.

She slowly opened the door.

Their eyes met. Agnes's jaw dropped. Shock, shame, and guilt overwhelmed her. After initial accusations by the daughter of abandonment and parental neglect, and attempts at self-justification by the mother, they embraced and settled down together for a few days of the winter school break. Mother and daughter took the time to reconnect as they shopped for a school uniform, shoes, and some essentials in preparation for Francinah's return to Taolome.

June of 1976 was a time of massive political turbulence in South Africa. Starting in the township of Soweto, young people in urban schools across the country erupted in an almost spontaneous revolt against the government's Afrikaans language policy in schools. The youth revolt, which left hundreds of schoolchildren dead, was to affect the tempo of change in South Africa for years to come.

In rural Taolome, as in most of rural South Africa, life went on pretty much undisturbed by the winds of change raging elsewhere in the country. So it was during her visit to Pretoria that Francinah found herself briefly caught up, with not a little surprise, in the turbulence of student resistance against apartheid education. She remembers running for safety during one of the skirmishes between the police and school kids. Having lived most of her life in the relative political stability of Chief Langa's chieftainship in Bakensberg and Taolome, Francinah's brief encounter with political strife in the urban centres never really affected her. "I was never involved in any of the politics," Francinah explained. She remained largely impervious to the political ferment raging in urban centres across the country.

The Sacred Dream: Called to be a Sangoma

It was during this brief visit to her mother that the dream from the ancestors came. Francinah dreamt that she was back at the Mthombeni household in a hut that was used for training new sangomas. In her dream, her paternal grandmother was there. Even though no words were exchanged, she knew when she awoke that this was a significant dream.

The dream was followed the next day by excruciating pains, as though needles were piercing Francinah's entire body. Her mother took her to the hospital. Western medicine could not find anything wrong with her, and she was sent back home.

Her mother, also a sangoma in her own right, asked a sangoma friend to "throw the bones" and examine her daughter. As the African saying goes, "*Ngaka ga e ikalafe*" (A doctor never cures himself/herself).

Francinah's destiny was written in the bones. "The paternal grandmother's spirit has come into your daughter," was the message they sent. The ancestors were calling her out for service. But she was only sixteen years of age and still at school, and so Agnes felt her daughter was too young to commit to such a heavy responsibility. She also knew that without education, her daughter would end up poor like her. Agnes's only option was to bargain with the ancestors to reschedule the date when her daughter would commence her vocation.

Mother and daughter set out on their trip back home to Taolome, in part to break the news to the rest of the family and in part to negotiate for more time to enable Francinah to further her schooling.

A date was arranged to covenant with the ancestors about allowing Francinah to finish her schooling. On the set day, she knelt at the gandelo while her mother communicated with the ancestors. The covenant was made with water, maize meal, snuff and a white chicken. These were presented to the ancestors at the gandelo (altar). The plea to the ancestors was a simple one: "We have heard you, and we do accept that Francinah will become a sangoma. Our plea is that she is still young. Please allow her to further her schooling. When she is old enough, she will enter the service of the ancestors."

It worked. The covenant was sealed with the blood of a chicken sacrificed for this purpose. Francinah's sickness disappeared, and she was able to further her schooling.

Following the successfully negotiated settlement for a temporary reprieve, this obligation remained like a cloud overhead. It was a debt Francinah would one day have to settle. It seemed somewhat unfair to her that the ancestors, who had lived their lives, were now wanting to steal hers and were ruling her from the grave.

Though one hurdle was out of the way – buying Francinah more time at school – she faced yet another: unrelenting poverty. Things did not change much, in spite of her desperate expedition to track down her mother in Pretoria. Her mother remained in Pretoria, made no attempt to maintain contact, and sent no supplies to alleviate Francinah's daily struggle to keep in school.

Thus by grade eight, Francinah had to make a life-defining choice. Staying in school meant that her younger brothers Phineas and Caiaphas stood less chance of getting an education. Theirs would be an inevitable one-way ticket to a life of poverty, repeating the appallingly poor economic fortunes of their parents. Moreover as boys, unlike girls, they would be expected to take care of their wives and children when they married. This was a social and cultural norm.

The only way for them to have a chance would be if Francinah left school to find a job and support them. She opted to do this, thus joining the millions of unsung women heroes who sacrifice themselves to give their younger siblings a better chance in life. Theirs is a story of talent that never had the opportunity to flourish.

Francinah was eighteen when she left school in 1977 without completing high school despite her obvious academic abilities. She headed to Ga-Rankuwa with a two-point agenda: to reconnect with her mother and to find a job. Migrating from a rural community to the city was a typical escape route from the grinding poverty of rural South Africa.

Once in Pretoria, Francinah had to get her official documentation in order, otherwise she could find herself arrested. Apartheid law prescribed that South Africa belonged to white people, and black people were assigned only thirteen percent of the land space, in what were called homelands. Passage into white South Africa was regulated by means of the pass document. The pass indicated whether one was permitted to be in urban South Africa or not. Blacks in urban townships were there because they were needed to provide manual labour to white South Africans. For such labour, the authorities, upon proof that one had found a job, would put an official stamp in the pass book that was also signed by the employer. The police could be expected to knock rudely on one's door in the dead of the night, looking to see if everyone sleeping in the house at the time had the necessary permit to be in that house.

Francinah would not be qualified because she was from Taolome in Mokopane. So she had to find a surrogate parent in the area who could "adopt" her, someone with the same surname who was willing to claim that Francinah was her child. This was one of the ways that blacks routinely worked around the laws of apartheid. Fortunately, there was a Baloyi in Makaunyane who agreed to do this favour, even though she was no relative of Francinah's. So the Baloyi surrogate matriarch accompanied Francinah to the Hammanskraal pass office, where she was able to get the necessary Section 10 stamp on her passbook. That way, she would be able to get a job in Pretoria.

The Second Coming of the Spirits

After arriving in Ga-Rankuwa, Francinah quickly found a job at the Yscor Club, thanks to relatives who helped. She was now a township girl and was quickly shedding the ways of the village. Ga-Rankuwa was very different from Taolome. It was home to thousands of people, cramped in row after row of small matchbox houses. A wider variety of languages were spoken than Francinah was accustomed to, with people from different parts of the country and even neighbouring countries having come to Pretoria for much the same reason she did: to find a job in South Africa's capital city of Pretoria. She had never lived in such a populous, congested and diverse environment.

Adding to Francinah's culture shock was the difference in lifestyle. People were less respectful of their elders than they had been in Taolome, more liberal in their dress and manners, and more indifferent to others.

As she settled in at her new job, the idea of becoming a sangoma was like an albatross that Francinah wanted to shake off. Life in Pretoria seemed to hold so much promise for self-development. She had better ideas about what she wanted for her life. She even changed jobs, taking employment as a cleaner with the Pretoria City Council. This is where she met and befriended Elizabeth Botjie, whom she fondly named Koko after her grandmother, because she was much older than her. They both worked as cleaners at the municipal caravan park in Pretoria.

One day Francinah visited Elizabeth at her home. That night she had a disturbing dream. In the dream, she was on her way to work and saw a very old man at the bus stop where she and Elizabeth usually took the bus to work. The old man walked towards where she was sleeping.

"He entered the yard of the house where I was staying. He turned to the house and opened the kitchen door and went straight to my bedroom. When he got there he changed my sleeping position. I was sleeping on my side, and he made me lie on my back. He shook my stomach once with both his hands and then disappeared. I woke up and opened my eyes. It was as if I had a snake inside of me that went up as if it wanted to come out of my mouth and then went down again. I could not sleep at all. Feeling this thing inside of me made me feel as if I was going crazy. I felt like a lunatic. I told my friend with whom I was visiting, and she gave me water to vomit. But that did not help."

Later that day, at Elizabeth's suggestion, Francinah went to see a prophet at a nearby church. It was an African Independent Church known as Kereke ya Postolo. The prophet took one look at her and said: "You are wasting my time. You know exactly what the problem is. You are running away from your calling, and the ancestors are very angry with you because you have changed your mind about the covenant you and your parents entered into with them. Go and do as your ancestors have requested." The prophet told Francinah that she had only ten days to live. She could either respond positively or die.

That got her attention. Francinah was scared. She wasted no time finding her mother and starting the arrangements to become a sangoma. Wanting a second opinion, Agnes connected her with other sangomas for a further diagnosis. They confirmed the prophet's word. "The ancestors are angry. If you do not *thwasa*, your life will never be the same again. The preparations must begin without further delay."

The word of the prophet and the word of the sangomas agreed: the ancestors were claiming her for their service, and she had to oblige. Or else something terrible would happen to her.

But first, Francinah had to appease the ancestors who appeared to be ready to show their displeasure at her disobedience. This required another session at the family gandelo. Another chicken sacrifice, with snuff and maize meal. More blood, a plea for forgiveness, and a covenant that this time the naughty girl would fully comply.

With that done, the next step was the actual training to be a sangoma. This was done back at the village in Taolome. It took several weeks of tutelage under experienced sangomas. In the end, six ancestral spirits who self-identified as her ancestors on both sides of her lineage made her body their home. They would be her spirit guides in the practice of her calling.

There was a seventh ancestral spirit, Mundau, that Francinah needed in order to complete the preparation for her sangoma calling. This was a water spirit, whom Francinah would receive at a river far from her village in Taolome. She had to travel to Giyani, some two hundred kilometres to the north-east, where suitably qualified sangomas would be able to perform the necessary rituals at the river.

Fortunately for Francinah, she had a distant cousin, Saina Makhubela, in Giyani who was happy to welcome her to the village and show her around. She helped her select the best sangoma principal who was popular with other initiates.

Saina herself was a member of the ten-million-strong Zion Christian Church (ZCC), an independent African church that traces its spiritual ancestry to the Azusa Street revival, but later branched off and embraced African ancestral spirituality. She accompanied Francinah throughout her initiation, which lasted several weeks. Francinah had to start by repeating the initiation she had done in Taolome because the Giyani principal was stricter and did not want to take anything for granted about how well the Mokopane sangomas had done their job.

Throughout the process, Saina was present as the next-of-kin, brewing the traditional beer that was necessary for such rituals. Because she was a member of the ZCC church, wearing the familiar ZCC badge, she had to endure the scorn of the African traditionalists and sangomas. In their view, Christianity of any stripe did not belong with African traditional practices of this sort. Saina's response to her accusers was, "Francinah is my cousin. I am her only relative in Giyani. I cannot leave her stranded, but must support her." Then she added words that would stay with Francinah for a long time: "How do you know, you sangomas who work with demons, what God may do with this child in the future? Maybe God will have mercy on her and save her, and she will serve God better than all of you!"

Francinah rejoiced at Saina's rock-solid support and comfort throughout these trying rituals, but wondered what those words meant.

Following the initiation at Giyani, Francinah was a fully-fledged sangoma, able to carry out all the traditional rituals including breaking curses and spells, helping women who wanted to keep their husband from straying, helping people who were going to court so that they were not found guilty, strengthening families and fortifying them from being bewitched, and unblocking barriers to progress and prosperity that came as a result of being bewitched. She soon found herself being invited to travel around the country as people heard of her powers to heal and protect people from witchcraft.

Her work as a sangoma brought in extra money, over and above her wages at work. So Francinah was now able to assist her brothers, Caiphus and Phineas, to further their schooling. Caiphus recalls how he used to travel from Taolome to visit Francinah in Pretoria and get some money for school. Even when he and his brother started working, they always knew they could rely on their big sister when they were out of pocket.

Influenced by her grandfather, Francinah believed that a good sangoma should neither kill nor cause harm to other people. "Since you can use muti to protect yourself from being bewitched, why would you want to kill someone who is seeking to harm you using muti? If you do, you may find yourself being alone in the world," her grandfather used to tell her.

4

A VISION AND A COMMISSION

Back to Ward 11, Kalafong Hospital, 1988.

Francinah looked up at the figure in front of her. His piercing eyes dug into her soul. *Who is he? Where is he from? What does he want from me?* These questions raced through her mind. Clearly he belonged with the gods, otherwise he would not have the power to order her ancestors to leave her in the way he did. But where did he fit in the spiritual scheme of things? His form, interestingly, was that of a human, though covered in shining light so that his features were barely discernible. So many questions went through Francinah's mind. She felt she was owed an explanation.

He approached her. Closer and closer he got to her until her spirit left her body, as though pulled out of her by a mighty force. The figure then turned, faced the opposite direction, and started to leave. As though pulled by some magnet, Francinah hung on to his shoulders with both hands. He looked up at the ceiling, and mysteriously it opened. So did the roof, as though it was obeying an order!

He led the way up through the roof with Francinah holding on to his shoulders, and they left the ward. She looked down at the grey roof beneath them as it receded, wondering what this strange dream meant.

Soon they were walking on air, heading eastward towards the rising sun. He was wearing white clothes, and Francinah was wearing her white hospital clothes and no shoes. They walked for a long time, facing the blue skies. Eventually the blue faded, and they came to a dark place. Beneath them was what appeared to be a very deep hole. To call it dark seemed like an understatement. It was intensely dark. The figure changed and appeared like fire. She followed the flame. Way down below, she could hear a cacophony of voices, people languishing in utter darkness. She was curious about them. Did she know any of them? How could anyone survive in a place like that! Suddenly from within the flame that she was following, a voice spoke to her for the first time: "If you look at those people who live in the dark and see the things in it, I will leave you here with them."

Francinah stopped trying to look, afraid of ending up in the same place. Soon she and the fiery presence emerged from that region of deep darkness, a place that appeared to her to be a place of desperate hopelessness. The presence moved on, and she quickly followed.

Some distance ahead of them she could see a most beautiful walled city, filled with light. So beautiful was it that even the ground seemed to be like a carpet rolled out for the people living there. They approached the gate.

Francinah was relieved. Finally, she reckoned, after travelling for what seemed like a very long time from her earthly sojourn and through the region of utter darkness, she was going to be able to rest in this beautiful city.

But suddenly as she approached the open gate, she found she was alone. And then a voice thundered from deep within the walls, from far inside this beautiful city. The power and force of the voice seemed to shake everything in sight. It addressed the thoughts in her mind. As a weary traveller, she wanted to find some rest in this beautiful city. But the voice said, "You cannot come through the gate! You do not have a resting place here."

Shame and utter despair overwhelmed her as the finality of the words sank in. She was not worthy to enter the beautiful city.

The Moment of Accountability

Suddenly, two men enveloped in brilliant white light were standing on each side of the gate. The man on the right was not very big. He was clad in a glowing white robe and had long hair, neatly combed back. The man on the left was huge and wore colourful glowing robes. His hair was short, his skin a darker shade than that of the first man. From within the city came voices of women and men singing: "Hallelujah!

Praise the Lord. Jesus is the King, Jesus is the Saviour, Jesus forgives. Hosanna! Glory!"

The man in white started to talk to Francinah. "You have sinned against God. You repeated your sin four times," he said.

Francinah knew that he was referring to her four abortions. It was as though the searchlight of heaven was pointing straight into the dark chambers of her soul, to the sin she had tried to sweep under the carpet of her consciousness.

He asked if she knew that she had sinned against God. Francinah acknowledged that she had indeed committed abortions. He pointed to the ground next to his left foot, where four lifeless babies lay in a heap. Francinah knew instinctively that these were her babies.

She started to weep. For the first time, she was seized by a sense of utter guilt about what she had done! She had killed real, fully formed children, not mere human tissue as she had imagined. Or as friends had made her believe. Even when the nurses said that she had lost a lot a blood, she had understood their words to be confirmation that it was not a human being that she had killed. This was a moment of reckoning for her. She was having to account for her actions before the heavens.

The mother in her started to reach out to touch the babies, to embrace and love the children she had mercilessly and mindlessly killed. As she moved towards them, the man in white robes warned her not to touch them. She tried to approach the man for mercy but was sternly told to stay where she was. She went back to where she had been standing, her eyes fixed on the children, tears flowing down her cheeks. Then the man stooped to separate the children and counted them, as if to make sure that she grasped the gravity of her sin.

"Who did such a cruel thing to these innocent children? Who killed them?" he asked. His words cut deep.

"I did, my Lord," she answered with immense guilt and shame. The weight of her sin was unbearable. The sacred space where she stood, at the door of the city of such splendour and glory, made her feel all the more small and unworthy.

"You must listen to me very carefully, because I want to talk to you. Since you have accepted your sins and showed remorse, God has forgiven you. He forgives you not only for your sin of abortion, but for all the other sins which were not shown to you. Because you have confessed your sin and have believed in me, I am cleansing you now from your sins," he said, using his hands to show how he was washing away her sins.

He continued, "I am filling you with my Spirit. You are now saved. I am sending you back to earth."

Francinah was relieved! She was given a second chance at life. Her sins were forgiven, and she could start afresh! She felt as though a huge burden of sin was rolled away from her shoulders, her dark past forgiven. She felt like she was now a new Francinah, cleansed both from the sins she knew she had committed and those she did not know about.

Her Assignment

The man in white robes continued to speak to her, "As you have sinned four times, I will give you four assignments to do on earth. First, you must pray for yourself. Second, you must pray for people in the world using only Jesus' name. Pray for everyone, even those who are not saved. Don't give them anything, and don't make them pay. When they believe in your prayer, all their problems will go away. Illness will be cured, and they will be blessed.

"Third, I am making you a prophet." Francinah imagined this to be the sort of prophet with which she was familiar, one who worked through the ancestral spirits. She knew this kind of prophecy was practised in some of the churches in the black townships. She recalled that earlier in her life when the spirits of the ancestors started to call her to their service, her friend Elizabeth had taken her to one of those churches. It was there that a prophet told her she would have to fulfil her covenant with her ancestors and become a sangoma. She was pleased because at least this assignment was not too far from what she was accustomed to.

The man saw her thoughts and sternly corrected her. That was not the kind of prophet he was speaking of. The type of prophets Francinah was thinking about were not of God. They were of the world and belonged to the kingdom of darkness.

Fourth, he told Francinah to go all over the world spreading the Word of God and what she had witnessed today.

Then turning back to the children, he said, "You see these children? They are not going to be thrown away, as you imagined. But their deaths will no longer be held against you, because your sins are forgiven."

Then he gave them to the man dressed in black, saying, "They are now on their father's account. From now on, they will trouble him day and night until he accepts me as his Saviour. If he does not accept me as his Saviour, these children will make him suffer until he comes here through death. He will also stand where you are standing now and give an account of his actions."

The man in colourful robes opened his arms and received the children, placing them on his lap, whereupon they disappeared.

"You are done now, Francinah. You can go back."

Before she could depart, the man in colourful robes took his turn to address her. When he opened his mouth to speak, the whole place shook. Fire came out of his mouth. Francinah was trembling.

He said, "Francinah, I am not sending you to other people. I am sending you to only one person, Joseph, the father of the four children you aborted. When you arrive at the hospital, you must ask the nurses to call him for you before he starts his shift at work. When he arrives, tell him everything that I am going to tell you. If he says you are lying and that you did not see God, he will die right on the spot. Tell him that his ways have angered God, and he must repent and accept Jesus into his life. Tell him that God knows that he has been giving you a hard time for the past ten years, and he does not regret it. Even as I speak to you, he is plotting to leave you and marry another woman, with whom he has been secretly involved for two years."

He continued to remind Francinah that God's mercy was upon her life, and that God would fight for her day and night.

He then repeated everything that the man in white had said, namely that she had been given four tasks to do. She was to start immediately when she got back to the hospital so that those at the hospital could be her witnesses.

Francinah's heart was sad at the prospect of walking away from the beautiful city to return to earth. She could hear the joy of the people inside. The two men turned to go back into the beautiful city and insisted that it was time for her to go back to the world, but she didn't want to go. She thought of a plan. She vaguely remembered the story of Abraham, reputed to be in heaven, with Lazarus the poor man at his bosom while Lazarus's uncaring rich neighbour was in hell. She had read this story in her Bible lessons at school. Maybe if she asked to see Abraham, they would let her go in.

Scared and uncertain of what she was asking for, with her hand covering her mouth, she thought to call out to the man in white robes. But she did not know his name. So she ventured a guess. "Jesus!" she called out.

"Jesus," she called out a second time, a bit louder. The man turned towards her. "Please Jesus, let me come inside so that I can see Abraham?"

He said, "My child, I can't let you inside now. I have sent you to the world. Go back and do what I have commanded you to do. You will come back again at the end of your days, and then you will not stand at the gate. You will come straight inside and see not only Abraham, but also many others who are sharing in my Father's eternal joy."

"Who are those happy ones, Lord?" Francinah asked.

"They are all those who received salvation while they were in the world, all those who had their sins forgiven. They are the ones who have been washed with the blood of Jesus Christ. You too, my child, are born again. Your sins have been forgiven. But now you must go back to the world."

Reluctantly, and not a little distraught, Francinah accepted the order to depart from the heavenly bliss and return to the world.

The journey back was instant. Francinah suddenly found herself back at the hospital, praying. This was strange, for prayer was not her thing. After all, she was a sangoma. But there she was, on her knees.

She was interceding for her boyfriend, the father of the aborted children pleading for mercy on his behalf so that he might see the light. The picture of the dark hole of the damned was haunting her. She could not imagine Joseph joining the company of the damned. She prayed for him to be given a chance, so that he could repent and find salvation in Christ.

After praying, Francinah tried to sleep. She felt a strange sensation, as though someone light, with feet as soft as that of a baby, was walking on her body, soothing her from the pain of the operation. She felt much better.

Then Francinah heard voices singing, praising the Lord, and praising God for her salvation, voices similar to the ones she heard in the beautiful city. They were quite close to her, but she could not see the people singing. While she felt a sense of belonging with this new community of worshippers, something was bothering her. What was she to do with the bones and muti that she kept back at her caravan park flat? These were not just physical objects; they were the stock-in-trade of her sangoma practice. They represented her previous life and the covenants she had entered into with her ancestors. They represented the religion of her ancestors. They were symbols of an intergenerational legacy passed on to her from her forebears. They were the way of life of her people.

She decided to raise the matter with the singers and asked them for advice about what to do with the sangoma paraphernalia: "Should I burn them?"

"Burn them, and put God first in your life," was the counsel of the singers.

Burn them, and put God first in your life. These words spelt the end of Francinah's sangoma identity and the beginning of her new identity in Christ. The end of one religion, the religion of her forebears, and the beginning of another, the way of Christ as her Lord and Saviour. Fire seemed an appropriate means by which to signal the end of the old and the beginning of the new. Her rite of passage from old to new would be through the flame of cleansing. From now on, Francinah would have to unlearn the old ways of life and learn what it means to put God first in her life.

Then the singers said they were going to give her a new song to mark her day of salvation – 1 August 1988. They would sing the tune, but God would give her the words to sing along. The words went:

> *I love Jesus,*
> *He forgave my sins.*
> *He had mercy on me,*
> *He is the King of kings.*
> *He is holy.*

As they sang the tune, Francinah sang the words. As she sang the last line "He is holy", they clapped their hands and praised the Lord loudly. Then they reminded her that it was time to start her assignment and tell the nurses about her experience and her healing.

A Dark Visitor

Francinah awoke with the drip still attached to her. Before she could get out of bed, she saw a very dark and tall man wearing black clothes sitting on a chair beside her bed where the ancestral spirits had been thrown down. His eyes were fiery red and his expression was one of rage. He seemed evil and accusing with his disapproving gaze fixed upon her. He was sitting between her bed and the nurses she wished to go and testify to. *Clearly this is the king of darkness; he is not sent from God*, she thought. She was reminded of the region of darkness through which she passed on her heavenly sojourn and figured this must be the ruler of that kingdom.

But why is he angry with me? Francinah wondered. Was it because she had "lost" the seven spirits that used to call her body their home? Interestingly, he was sitting at the exact spot where all seven had crashed to the floor and disappeared. It was as if the spirits had gone to report to him, and he had come to verify whether Francinah, who had been their home for six years, had truly become a no-entry zone for them.

Or was he angry because Francinah was no longer a sangoma, having made a 180 degree turn away from the practice? Or maybe he resented the very idea that she had become a Christian, having crossed the floor from being a champion of the sangoma practice to being a messenger of the gospel of Jesus Christ? Whatever the cause of his fury, Francinah felt protected in Christ and knew no harm would befall her. She was not going back to her previous life.

Just then a hymn welled up within her, one that she remembered from her school days. She began to sing it:

Ke gaugetswe ke Mong wa ka	My Lord had mercy on me
ka gobane ga nka ka mo nyaka	Because I never sought after him
ke soko le sa ntshwaneleng	it is grace I did not deserve
Yena e a nkgogileng	He drew me to himself
ke gona bjalo ke thabang	I can now rejoice
ka Jesu e a ntshokelwang	because of Jesus who had mercy on me
Tsuo e thata le go tiwa	Misery and punishment
Ke tsona tse di ntebaneng	is what awaited me

Eupsa ka na ka hlatswiwa	But I was washed
ka madi a ntsholegetseng	by the blood that was spilt for me
Me bjalo nka leboga mang	Who then can I thank?
Ke Jesu e a ntshokelwang	Only Jesus who had mercy on me

Just as Francinah sang the line, "I was washed by the blood that was spilt for me", the "man" literally flew out of the ward, chair and all! Francinah was awed by the impact the blood of Jesus had on him. Just then she heard the joyful singing of the angels again: "Hallelujah! You have overcome the evil one. Now you can begin the work of the Lord." They also told her that after her surgery she should not drink cold water, but only warm or hot water for three days.

At the end of the rather dramatic exorcism Francinah had experienced earlier that evening, she had felt that she was owed an explanation. She now felt answered. Indeed, more than answered. She now knew that the stranger who had pulled the ancestral spirits out of her as with a powerful magnet and smashed them on the floor was Jesus Christ, and that he is Lord, in heaven and on earth. He is sovereign over all. That is why he had the power to expel her ancestors from her and then proceeded to show her the heavenly city.

The biblical text began to make sense:

> Therefore God exalted him to the highest place
> and gave him the name that is above every name,
> that at the name of Jesus every knee should bow,
> in heaven and on earth and under the earth,
> and every tongue acknowledge that Jesus Christ is Lord,
> to the glory of God the Father. (Phil 2:9–11)

Over the years of Francinah's ministry, she would learn to use the power and authority of the name of Jesus when she dealt with those possessed by demons. As she prayed for other sangomas enslaved by ancestral spirits as she had been, she would remember Jesus' words: "These signs will accompany those who believe: In my name they will drive out demons" (Mark 16:17).

Francinah also knows the place of ancestral spirits in relation to the Kingdom of Heaven. For generations her family, and indeed her community, had understood ancestors as intermediaries between the living and the Creator. To be sure, her people never worshipped them as God, but they would sacrifice animals to appease them or enter into covenants with them, as she had done. Those who combined African traditional beliefs and Christianity would say, "*Re rapela Modimo le badimo*" (We pray to God and the ancestors). Now Francinah knew that this part of the African traditional belief system is displeasing to God. The mediator role between God and people is reserved for Christ alone. Only he who had no sin was chosen to do it, having paid the ultimate price to atone for the sins of humankind: "For there is one God and one mediator between God and mankind, the man Christ Jesus, who gave himself as a ransom for all people. This has now been witnessed to at the proper time" (1 Timothy 2:5–6).

Francinah was grateful to God that she had been enabled to see and make the choice between true religion and false. She was now following the one who said: "I am the way and the truth and the life. No one comes to the Father except through me" (John 14:6).

Francinah also understood that the reason Jesus came to her bedside in hospital was because she had a case to answer in the court of heaven for the babies she aborted. While it is generally held that a foetus is not really a human being and can be discarded at will, she now understood that before God, human life at any stage is precious. For that reason, her sin of abortion was like murder and indeed a grievous sin before God.

Ever since abortion was legalized in 1997 in South Africa (as a victory for those who consider it a fundamental feminist right) the numbers of abortions done in public hospitals has grown to a staggering 155,624 (2001 figures), with more than half performed on girls under eighteen years of age.[1]

Francinah felt answered about the nature of the war between the kingdom of darkness and the kingdom of the light and the place of the blood of Jesus as a game-changer in that battle. The hasty and undignified flight of the prince of darkness at the mere singing of a song about the blood of Jesus taught her an important truth about spiritual warfare.

---

[1] Jimmy Seepe, "Shocking Abortion Figures", Health Systems Trust, 13 May 2001, accessed 5 May 2016, http://www.hst.org.za/news/shocking-abortion-figures

The battle against evil cannot be won by mere human effort, or by rational means. Evil is a kingdom with a king. Those who seek to fight its many manifestations cannot do so in their own power, but would be well advised to rely in the power of God.

Finally, Francinah felt more than answered as she pondered the amazing love of the God who loved a sinner like herself – a sinner who killed innocent babies and practised a cult that God found so sinful and unacceptable. How could she ever have known that this ancestral religious practice, though deeply ingrained in her culture, was wrong unless Jesus himself had shown her? Francinah felt indeed favoured among sangomas and loved for no apparent reason she could think of. God had forgiven her sins and saved her from ending up in the place of the damned, where she would spend an eternity of sheer hell.

Further, not only did God love her, he loved all sinners and had given her an assignment to tell other sinners like herself about his unmerited love for them. She could say with St Paul: "I am obligated both to Greeks and non-Greeks, both to wise and the foolish. That is why I am so eager to preach the gospel also to you who are in Rome. For I am not ashamed of the gospel, because it is the power of God that brings salvation to everyone who believes" (Rom 1:14–16).

Ministry Begins

Francinah felt thankful and truly blessed as she got out of bed.

By now she felt thirsty and longed for some water. Then she remembered that the angels had warned her not to drink cold water because of her operation. As she moved towards the nurses, she could see a white cloud enveloping her. She asked the nurses for hot water, and they pointed her to a basin with a tap where she could get hot water. After helping herself to a cup of hot water, she made her way back to her bed. Just then she heard a voice from within the cloud that was covering her, visible only to herself, saying, "Go and tell the nurses about what you saw." Francinah went back to them and told them that she had seen Jesus and that God had sent her to preach the gospel. They thought she had lost it. Having been admitted into the hospital as a sangoma, she was now claiming that she had seen Jesus and God had sent her! They were convinced she was crazy.

Francinah did not argue with them but made her way back to her bed. As she was about to climb onto her bed, the voice in the cloud said to go back and tell them again.

She obeyed. Again she was dismissed and herded back to her bed.

A third time Francinah was told to tell them. The same response from the nurses awaited her. The voice then told her that since the nurses did not wish to listen, she was to take off the IV drips and leave the hospital to pray at a nearby hill. She ripped off the drip. Blood started to flow, making a mess. This only added to the nurses' conviction that she had gone mad. They called security to restrain her so that she could not leave the hospital. She returned to her bed.

As Francinah lay in bed, the voice in the cloud gave her a word for the sick girl lying on the fourth bed from hers. "That girl will be going to theatre tomorrow. She won't make it; she will die. Go to her and tell her to believe in God. If she does, she will be healed and not even go to theatre. When the sun rises, she will be able to get out of bed and sit unassisted."

Francinah got out of bed, with the cloud still surrounding her, and gingerly made her way to that girl. She could feel the eyes of the nurses following her, monitoring what she was up to. The girl was about twenty years old, and really ill. She lay helpless and frail.

Francinah greeted her and told her to believe in Jesus Christ and God and she would be healed. The girl accepted and believed.

The nurse rebuked Francinah for being a busybody and disturbing other patients. She was told to lie in bed and rest, as she hadn't had much rest since the operation.

Francinah pitied the nurse. "I used to be like you, fighting against anyone who spoke to me about God," she said. "Today God has taken control of my life, and I am doing what he has sent me to do. Do you see this cloud that is surrounding me?"

"No. You are crazy. There is no cloud here," replied the nurse.

"If you could see this cloud, you would not be calling me crazy. You would know that I am doing God's work," Francinah replied.

The nurse's curiosity was stirred. She invited Francinah to come tell her and her colleagues in the ward about it. Francinah happily obliged.

She told them everything she experienced, from the time her ancestors were exorcized to her trip to the beautiful city and back! She also told them to call Joseph for her so that she could tell him what the angel said regarding the aborted children. They listened attentively. Whether they listened because they were inwardly convicted by her words or simply entertained by her out-of-this-world fantasies, she could not tell.

When Francinah was done, they thanked her and appeared softened.

Then they said, "Francinah, there are two things we won't let you do for God. We won't let you leave this hospital to go and pray on the mountain. If we do, we will be in trouble with the hospital authorities for letting you leave. We might end up in jail. Second, we will not call Joseph to come here because when he hears that you are in hospital, he will think you are dying and wish to say your final words to him. He might be frightened and cause an accident on his way to the hospital. Talking to Joseph about the message from God will have to wait till you are discharged from the hospital. Please ask God to forgive us."

The nurses now encouraged Francinah to get some sleep, since she had not had much rest since the operation. She asked to be allowed to go to the ladies' room to pray. There Francinah thanked God for his forgiveness and the salvation of her soul. Like Saul who was killing innocent people, she had killed innocent babies. She asked God to save young girls who fell into the trap of having abortions like she used to.

Satisfied after praying, Francinah proceeded to her bed and slept.

About six to eight doctors came in and woke her up, curious about the report they heard from the nurses. They remarked that she appeared calm and stable and wondered what had happened. They were impressed when she told them that she was not in any pain. They decided to put her back on the drip, just in case, and so they could monitor her before she was discharged.

A nurse proceeded to fill out some file on Francinah's condition and check her mental state.

"What is your date of birth?" she asked.

"1960 on 4 February," Francinah replied.

"Marital status?"

"Not married."

"Do you have any children? How many girls and boys and what are their dates of birth?"

"I have three children, two girls and one boy," Francinah replied. "My firstborn is a girl, who was born on the 6th of January 1978. My second born is a boy, born on the 17th of June 1979. My last born is a girl, who was born on the 14th of April 1982."

"Where do you work?" asked the nurse.

"I work for the city council of Pretoria."

The nurse was satisfied that Francinah was not mentally confused. Her line of questioning changed. "Do you know what happened to you?"

"Yes I know what happened to me," Francinah replied. "I got saved."

"What are you going to do about being a traditional healer?"

"I am going to burn everything that has to do with being a sangoma healer when I get home."

"Will the sangoma community to which you belong not be against that?"

"I do not owe them anything," Francinah replied.

"You must never turn against God," the nurse said. "A lot of people died at the hospital, but you have made it."

"I will never leave God nor forget what he did for me," Francinah replied.

The following day, the girl on the fourth bed was healed and did not have to go for an operation. She testified that it was because Francinah spoke to her the night before and told her about Jesus. When some nurses said that Francinah was crazy, she defended her and shared her testimony. She told them how when Francinah came to her the night before, she thought Francinah was going to give her a final message for her family, as she thought Francinah was dying. But the reverse was true. Francinah came to give her life!

Francinah stayed another full day at the hospital before she was discharged.

5

A NEW LIFE AND A NEW MISSION

Francinah was an active, charming extrovert, well-liked by her colleagues. So when she arrived back at work from hospital around lunchtime on Wednesday the 3rd August 1988, her colleagues were very happy to see her. Everyone wanted to talk and hear how she was, because when she had left in the ambulance earlier that week, she had been so ill she could barely walk. She had to be helped into the ambulance. But they were surprised that the usually warm and chatty Francinah was now detached and taciturn. She kept quiet, shivering a bit, with her head bowed, as her colleagues asked questions to try to find out what was going on. Even her best friend and confidant, Elizabeth Botjie, began to worry. She took her aside to their favourite spot in the municipal caravan park, away from the others.

"You have changed. You are never this quiet. Why are you not speaking to the people? Tell me what happened to you?" asked Elizabeth.

For the first time Francinah lifted her head, holding and keeping Elizabeth in her gaze.

"I am no longer a sangoma. I am saved."

"You are what!?" Elizabeth was stunned as she looked at her friend, who was still shaking and quite clearly shook up by whatever it was she had been through.

"I am saved. My ancestors were taken out before my very eyes."

Francinah proceeded to take Elizabeth through the drama of the past forty hours. From her encounter with Jesus in Ward 11 to her deliverance, her journey via hell to heaven, her standing at the gates of heaven and giving an account for the lifeless bodies of her aborted children, receiving forgiveness and the new calling and assignment she had received. Francinah gave every detail of it while Elizabeth listened without interruptions, awestruck by the marvel of it all.

"And now, I still hear the heavenly voices of the angels singing and praising God that I am saved. I cannot hear when people speak to me. I also see people as if we are separated by a transparent glass. That is why I could not hear the colleagues; I could only see them moving their lips."

Elizabeth was speechless at the testimony of her friend, awestruck at the amazing grace that God had shown to one who had been so far from Christianity, a sangoma who had aborted so many children.

Elizabeth thought about her own faith. Before she met Francinah, she had been a religious and God-fearing woman. Elizabeth had tried to interest Francinah in the things of God, but to no avail. The calling of the ancestors on Francinah's life had made things worse, and Elizabeth had drifted away from the church. In the end, the bond of their friendship made Elizabeth lose all connection with the church as she stood by Francinah throughout her journey as a sangoma. Now her friend was not only saved, she had received another calling for her life: to be a preacher of the gospel of Christ. Elizabeth decided there and then to be the first convert. She made a decision to rededicate her life to Christ. As they had been soul mates outside the Christian faith, so they became soul mates on the journey of serving Christ.

Francinah remained in "spiritual quarantine" for almost two months, seeing people as though separated by a glass and only hearing people when they spoke about God. For some people, this was an indication that she was somehow mentally disturbed. Some relatives even suggested taking her to a sangoma, which Francinah fiercely resisted.

The brand of religion that Francinah came out of hospital with can broadly be called evangelicalism. This word signifies a cluster of beliefs that includes a personal decision to turn away from one's sinful past in order to be a devoted follower of Christ. A good 25 percent of the South African Christian community would self-identify as evangelical, including those who prefer the designation Pentecostal or Charismatic.[1]

---

[1] L. Kretzschmar and M. Ntlha, *Looking Back, Moving Forward: Reflections by South African Evangelicals* (Johannesburg: TEASA, 2005), 79.

Francinah's conversion to the faith was unencumbered by much of Christianity's baggage. Unlike many people in South Africa who come to faith from a background of Christian nominalism, she had no history of Christian socialization. Francinah belongs to that rare group of Christians who, like the Apostle Paul, were evangelized by Jesus Christ himself and started their Christian journey with a high level of clarity about what they are called to do.

Following her operation and heavenly vision, Francinah immediately set about working out the implications of her new faith and carrying out her assignment.

She pondered on the rather bizarre message she was to deliver to her boyfriend. "I have been to heaven and back and seen Jesus and the angels. He said to tell you, 'Unless you repent, you will also stand before God and account for your sins one day.' And if you don't believe what I am telling you, they'll kill you!"

She wondered how this message would land in Joseph's ears.

She did not know it at the time, but delivering messages like this is part of evangelical Christianity around the world. Once you have been "born again", to use evangelical language, you are expected to share your faith with others, starting with those closest to you. It is this tenet of evangelical belief that accounts for their numerical growth, the idea of "each one teach one", or one-on-one evangelism.

Joseph's eyes opened wide as he listened to the story of her ordeal at the hospital, as well as her journey to the heavens and back. He wasn't sure what to make of it. Knowing that Francinah was not one to make jokes like this, he gave her the benefit of the doubt.

What further unsettled him was that Francinah had been informed of his secret plan to marry another woman. He had managed to conceal it from her in the past.

When Francinah realized that Joseph was set on continuing with his other relationship, they agreed to end their affair.

Facing Family

Francinah's religion before that eventful Monday evening in August 1988 was African traditional religion. Her family was the cradle in which she was called and formed as a sangoma. How would they receive her story? Would they reject her or censure her in some way? She did not know, but would soon find out. With some trepidation, she decided to take the bull by the horns and start with her mother.

Francinah was discharged from the hospital on the Wednesday following her admission earlier that week. By Thursday, she had already delivered Joseph's message. Her next mission was to face her mother.

That Friday, Francinah took a taxi and headed towards her mother's place just outside Winterveldt, Pretoria, to spend the weekend with her.

When she got to Agnes's house, Francinah could not bring herself to break the news. What gave her cold feet was that she knew her mother was very strict and traditional in her outlook. As far as Agnes was concerned, her daughter came home to convalesce following her operation and maybe also to level with her about her abortions. So after the welcoming preliminaries, Agnes went straight to the point: "I must talk to the ancestors to intercede for you." She gave Francinah no time to think and proceeded to the gandelo for the ritual of *go phasa badimo*, to intercede and ask for forgiveness from the ancestors for whatever mischief her daughter might have done. Agnes mixed her concoction at the gandelo, expecting Francinah to come kneel by her side as was her usual practice.

Francinah did not move. She kept thinking: *Those ancestors who couldn't even put up a fight against Jesus at the hospital, how could they be of any use?* Agnes could see that something about her daughter had changed, but she did not know what.

"Come and kneel before the ancestors!" she beckoned for her daughter to join her, puzzled at her rebellion. Francinah did not say a word, nor did she approach the gandelo. Agnes proceeded to intercede for her, asking the ancestors to forgive Francinah for her abortion. She did not know that there were actually four abortions to intercede for. With the ritual completed, the conversation returned to more mundane matters.

Finally, Francinah managed to master the courage to confront her mother.

"There is something I need to tell you," she said, motioning to her mother to take a seat. As she sat down, Agnes knew that something serious was coming. Francinah started with the abortions, telling her mother that the final count was four by the time she went in for the operation earlier that week. Then she related the story of how she had lost the spirits of her ancestors that had lived in her since her induction as a sangoma.

Agnes was speechless as she listened to her daughter tell the story of Jesus casting out the spirits of the ancestors. As if that was not enough drama, the story continued to play out in the heavens, where her daughter was confronted with the evil of her deeds and send back to earth with a mission from God.

Francinah was pleasantly surprised that her mother listened patiently without interrupting her. She wondered what she was thinking.

When it was Agnes's turn to respond, she chose her words guardedly. "*Re a le utlwa. Ke lena le boneng. Ke lena le utlwileng*" (I hear you. You are the one who saw, and you are the one who heard).

Francinah was relieved that the reception was a positive one, even though Agnes's response was loaded. First, Agnes granted that her daughter had indeed experienced what she claimed. Someone with a more rationalist mind-set might have rejected all this as nonsensical. For African people in general, however, the spirit world is as real as the natural world. One has to travel far and wide to find a serious and committed African atheist. For better or worse, Africans know too much of the reality of the spirit world to be atheists. So at least Francinah did not have to worry about arguing the case for the reality of the other world, at least not to her mother.

However, the other side of Agnes's response was that the revelation was for Francinah alone. She was the naughty girl who had committed the hideous deeds of abortion. "For her, it was like a punishment for my deeds," explained Francinah. Taking this view meant that Francinah could follow her calling, without opposition from her mother.

As she rounded off her response to her daughter, Agnes wished her well. "You must stick with your new calling and not come back to us and our ways of badimo (ancestors). Pray for us that we may join you, but you must not come back to us."

Francinah was delighted at this ray of hope that suggested that her mother was open to even considering turning her back on badimo to follow Christ with her.

Agnes wanted to know what Francinah was going to do with her sangoma paraphernalia, all the stuff that was part of a sangoma's toolkit in the exercise of her trade.

"I will burn all that. I have to destroy everything because it represents my covenant with badimo, the ancestors. I must burn it to signal that my covenant with them has come to an end. Jesus told me that I must have nothing to do with badimo again. I am now redeemed and saved from the ways of darkness. I am now called to preach his gospel."

This response took Agnes by surprise. The ancestors would surely disapprove. But she knew her daughter well enough to realize she had made up her mind. It would be futile to try to stop her.

They spent the rest of Francinah's visit talking about other things and avoiding the "elephant in the room", which was what to do with Francinah's gandelo.

Francinah proceeded to do as she had said several days later, accompanied by Christians she had met and started to befriend after they heard her testimony. She burnt the muti that she kept at the caravan park where she stayed on weekdays while she was working, going home only on weekends. The muti at her mother's home would have to wait till later.

Her father was the next stop. He too had to know that Francinah was no longer a sangoma. After all, he had fully supported her throughout her initiation, training, and induction as a sangoma. She made arrangements to travel back to the village of Bakensberg where her father lived and then on to Taolome where her maternal grandparents lived so she could tell them. But this journey had to wait till the following month, September, when Francinah's annual leave was due.

Samuel listened attentively from beginning to the end as his daughter told the story of her abortions, her spiritual encounter with Jesus, and her heavenly sojourn. Like Agnes, he had no trouble believing his daughter's amazing testimony.

Samuel responded, "*Re a go lebohisa. Tse tsa badimo di boima. Nna ke ya ho lokolla, o latelle morena Jesu moraho*" (I am happy for you. The calling of the ancestors is a heavy matter. I release you to follow Jesus). Years earlier, he himself had ceased to practise as a sangoma and had donated his sangoma garments to his daughter.

Samuel wished his daughter well and added that if anyone questioned her choice to leave the ancestor cult behind, she must refer them to him. He probably said this because he anticipated that Francinah was going to have a tough time explaining matters to her maternal grandparents, who were more steeped in tradition.

She then went to the homestead of the maternal grandparents in Taolome. After the initial excitement of welcoming her after a long absence from the village, the grandparents finally settled down, waiting to hear the reason for this visit from the city girl.

Francinah narrated the whole story, the abortions, her encounter with Jesus, her visit to the heavens, the message to Joseph, and her new mission to preach the gospel. They were glued to their chairs, amazed at what they were hearing from their granddaughter.

After hearing her out, her grandfather, said, "I hear you, my grandchild." Being the more practical sort, he started pondering the implications of this heavenly vision. He had just come from the veld where he had been collecting some muti for use in curing the sick. He continued, "Now that they said you must no longer work with *badimo* (ancestors) and *dihlare* (muti), what are you going to do for the sick who come to you for help?"

"I will pray to God for them, and God will heal them. I am no longer going to use badimo," Francinah replied.

Upon hearing this, the grandfather chuckled. Seizing the opportunity to be among the first to benefit from his granddaughter's prayer ministry, he threw down the gauntlet: "*Ngwana ngwanaka, wa tla wa fitlha pila. Ke khale ke tshwenywa ke maoto, a bohloko! Nke o nthapelle lenna.*" (You did well to come and visit us, my granddaughter. I have pains in my feet. Start with me. Please pray for me.)

Francinah prayed for him, and sure enough, he was instantly healed. He was very happy that he was now going to be able to walk without much pain. He also wished Francinah well in her new religion, but felt it was not for him.

This was her first month in the faith. Having heard her testimony, her grandparents and all her cousins supported her in her new found faith and her mission to preach the gospel.

Mission in the Village

Francinah took all the money she had in the bank and bought a loudhailer (megaphone) she could use to begin her mission of preaching the gospel as instructed in her vision. At that time, there was hardly any evangelical, born-again church in Taolome, and so during her three weeks' leave, Francinah started holding an open air service every evening as people were coming back from work.

She would start by singing a chorus in the streets as she made her way to an open space not far from her grandparents' homestead. A crowd would begin to gather and soon numbered a couple of hundred. Most of the people knew Francinah because she had grown up in the village. They knew she had been with them in the *koma* – the traditional initial school for young girls preparing for adulthood. They also knew that she had been a sangoma. So in the services, Francinah would share her testimony as a converted sangoma, speaking about the sin of abortion and her encounter with Jesus at the hospital. She also spoke about the judgment that awaits all who reject the saving message of Christ and prefer to cling to the idols of their own culture.

For many, this was the first time they heard the gospel preached with such clarity and power. Francinah also prayed for the sick, and many were healed. The services would go on until midnight.

On one of the evenings when she was preaching, Francinah said: "I no longer use badimo or dihlare, but no one will ever bewitch me. My protection is only in Jesus Christ."

She said this because she knew some of those listening were witches in the village. After midnight that evening, as the people dispersed, Francinah started walking home with her cousin. The cousin was anxious, "My sister, you have caused us trouble. Now you have invited the witches of this village to come to our house to bewitch us. They will surely come!"

"No, they will not come," countered Francinah. "Do you think they will come to our place even when I told them that Jesus is stronger than they are? They will never come!" In her mind, Francinah was convinced they wouldn't dare.

She was wrong. At around two in the morning, she was awakened by a slight movement at the door. The door cracked open, just a little bit. In walked five women through that slight opening, which could not have been a centimetre wide. They filed in one by one, lining up along the wall. Francinah kept silent. In the moonlit room, she could recognize who they were because she had grown up in this village. After a short pause, one of them approached the bed on which she was sleeping.

Vinolia, the cousin with whom Francinah normally shared the bed, had made it clear to her when they got to home that evening that she was going to sleep on the floor, so that when the witches came that night, they would not get confused and harm her by mistake. Francinah had provoked them, and she would have to deal with the consequences.

The witch who approached the bed attempted to put *segateledi* on Francinah, a nightmarish dream that leaves one with a sense of being utterly helpless, unable to scream for help or react in anyway.

Francinah boldly and emphatically spoke, "In Jesus name!"

Instantly the witch was flung back, hitting hard against the wall and letting out a deep groan.

The witches whispered to the next witch to approach. Again Francinah called out the name of Jesus, with the same result. There was a thud as this witch too shot back against the wall, and a groan. The same fate awaited all five witches.

When it became clear to them that they were not prevailing in their mission, they started to file back out, as if in a choreographed queue, through the slightly opened door. As they left, Francinah looked through the window and watched as they disappeared into one of the huts belonging to a relative who was a notorious witch.

The following evening, the witches were not in the service, but their daughters were. Francinah spoke about the incident: "Last night, I was visited by some witches, but they were defeated by the power of God. Now I know that witches all work with their children and wake them up at night to accompany them on some of their evil assignments. Today I am going to pray for those whose mothers are witches. From tonight, when they wake you up in the middle of the night for their nightly missions, you will not wake up, in Jesus name!" She then proceeded to pray for them.

A few days later, the witches confronted Francinah: "Take your bags and leave this village. What kind of church is this of yours? Ever since you came here to preach, our children no longer respond to us when we wake them up at night. None of the churches that have been in this community for a long time have ever given us any such problems. Pack your bags and leave!"

Francinah did just that, for her leave was ending and she still wanted to make one final stop in Giyani, Limpopo, before she had to return to work in Pretoria. Giyani was where she had been finally inducted as a sangoma and had covenanted with the Mundau water spirit.

Francinah's first month as a Christian had borne much fruit in Taolome. Many had come to believe on the Lord Jesus Christ. But because she herself was a new believer and not yet fully discipled, she did not make any arrangement for what would happen to the new believers that she had led to Christ after she left the village. Many went back to their old ways.

Years later, Francinah visited the village of Taolome again on the occasion of a cousin's wedding. As people were milling around the family homestead celebrating the initial steps of a traditional wedding and the paying of lobola (dowry), someone caught Francinah's attention. A slightly tipsy man named Monamodi, looking a bit like a hobo ravaged by alcohol abuse, was talking to friends and some family members around the fire.

"You know here in the Baloyi clan, years ago there was a powerful woman preacher who started evening services in this village," he said. "She really taught us about God, and many of us started to follow Christ. But she disappeared, and I don't know where she went or why she left us. Now look at me. I am a drunkard, and my life is wasting away. I believe if her church had continued in this village, I would not be like this. Can anyone tell me where that powerful preacher went to?"

The man spoke with a sobering earnestness that belied the generous helping of alcohol he had consumed, while puffing away at his cigarette.

What he said cut Francinah to her core. "Who is the women you are talking about? Would you recognize her?" Francinah asked, unable to hide her curiosity.

"Yes I think so. I know that she was a Baloyi. I was told she was Fire's sister. That is why I am asking around here in the Baloyi clan. I am hoping that someone might be able to tell me where that preacher is."

Fire was the nickname given to Francinah's younger brother Phineas. Francinah owned up, "I am the person you are talking about. I am Fire's sister."

She knew that she had blundered in not making any arrangements for the nurture of the new believers. She encouraged Monamodi to join one of the evangelical churches in greater Bakensberg, assuring him that it was not too late to recommit his life to Christ.

From Taolome to Giyani

While in Giyani, Francinah decided to call in at the home of the sangoma principal who initiated her, for she wanted to make sure that she had covered all the bases where she had been initiated into the different levels of the sangoma cult. She asked her aunt, Saina Makhubela to accompany her. Auntie Saina was happy to do so as she had been there with Francinah when she was initiated and received the Mundau water spirit. Saina recalled having warned the sangomas that God might surprise all of them and save Francinah, calling her into his service. That day had come, and Saina wanted to be there to see the sangomas' faces when they heard the news.

As she had done with other significant people in her life, Francinah gave her full testimony to her mentor in Giyani. She also checked with her that she had no outstanding debts for her initiation. Because she knew about covenants with ancestor spirits, Francinah was aware that if spiritual covenants are not completely broken, a door is left open for spiritual attack or bondage in the future. Not paying fees that had been agreed upon give the spirits a legitimate claim over you. Thankfully, Francinah was paid up and had no outstanding debts for her initiation as a sangoma.

Francinah's mentor was thankful that she had come to inform her personally, so that she did not have to hear Francinah's story through hearsay.

Like Francinah's sangoma parents and grandparents, the Giyani sangoma's parting words to Francinah were, "We are happy for you. Make sure that you stay with Christ and Christianity for good. Do not come back to us and the ancestors. Pray for us that we too may be able to follow you where you are and follow your Christ."

The unanimity of all the sangomas who had mentored Francinah in wishing her well in her faith and encouraging her never to return is rather intriguing. One would have expected them to be hostile towards a "defector" and bemoan her disloyalty to the traditional cause. Yet they all appeared to express a desire to escape the sangoma fold themselves, and all asked her to pray for their release. It was as if some bondage prevented them from bolting for freedom.

For her part, Auntie Saina eventually made up her mind to follow Francinah in her new faith. Her husband followed suit, as did many other family members and relatives who witnessed Francinah's life change for the better before their very eyes.

Having levelled with her sangoma mentors, parents, and grandparents and the extended family, including her home village in Taolome, Francinah now felt ready to begin the adventure of her new calling as a preacher of the Christian gospel.

Church Life

Francinah's entry into the Christian faith was dramatic and unencumbered by Christian socialization. She knew almost nothing about the do's and don'ts of church life. But Christian discipleship is hardly possible without a firm grounding in a local community of sisters and brothers who are also followers of Christ, determined to grow in their faith and service to their Master Jesus Christ.

Thankfully, the first born-again believer Francinah met after her conversion was Mr Moloba, a colleague who worked with her as a messenger at the municipality. When Francinah was discharged from hospital, she called Joseph and asked him to send her some clothing.

Joseph arranged for Mr Moloba to deliver them. As a messenger, he could easily include a stop at Kalafong Hospital in his errands. He happened to be a member of the Assemblies of God. Francinah wasted no time sharing her new faith with him. Knowing her reputation as a sangoma, Mr Moloba was quite puzzled and rather unconvinced. He decided to quiz her on the basics of the Christian faith to satisfy himself that she had turned her back on being a sangoma and was now committed to being a follower of Christ. She easily passed her test.

The believer who introduced Francinah to church was Godfrey Straight. Francinah had visited a cousin, Martha, in Ga-Rankuwa. Upon hearing her testimony, Martha, not a Christian herself, thought that what Francinah was saying was similar to what her neighbour Godfrey used to tell her. So she figured Godfrey could explain more to Francinah about the Christian life. The connection was made, and soon Francinah started going to the same church as Godfrey. It was an Alliance church near Winterveldt, in a part of Mabopane called Beirut.

Very early one Sunday morning, at about 4:00 a.m., Francinah was awakened by a strange voice saying, "Today you must not go to work. This is the day of your baptism."

She was stunned. She knew the voice was God's, but who would baptize her? She had not made any arrangements with anyone. So she enquired of the Lord about it. The inner voice of the Spirit said, "Godfrey will help you. Go and tell him that today is the day of your baptism. He will know what to do."

By 6:00 a.m. that morning, Francinah was knocking at Godfrey's home in Ga-Rankuwa.

"Who is it?" enquired a voice from inside. It was Godfrey.

"Francinah," she replied.

"Is there a problem? Why are you here so early?"

"Open the door; I will explain."

Once inside the house, she explained the reason for the early morning visit. Puzzled, Godfrey didn't know what to do, because there was no baptism planned for that day at the church.

"But Francinah, baptism services are arranged well in advance!" he said.

"I don't know these things, except that God said I must tell you that this is the day for my baptism."

After thinking about it briefly, Godfrey disappeared to the bedroom to confer with his wife. They both decided the best course of action was to go to church early and see what could be arranged. Upon arrival at the church, they found that Pastor Simelane, an elderly man from another Alliance church, was already there. He had been woken up that morning by the Lord saying, "You must not go to your church today. Go to the Alliance church in Beirut. There is someone there I want you to baptize for me."

On arriving at the church, Pastor Simelane asked the believers who were already gathered there about who he was meant to baptize. They knew nothing about it as there were no baptisms planned for that day. While they are talking, Francinah and Godfrey walked in. Pastor Simelane saw her and knew instinctively that she was the one. He interrupted Godfrey as he started to explain the situation. "Say no more," he said. "Let's go to the river for the baptism. The Lord has spoken to me about you. The rest I will hear on the way." They prayed and thanked the Lord and went to the nearby river that flows between Boekenhout and Lebanon, in the urban sprawl called Mabopane. They were accompanied by Pastor Maduna and other believers.

Francinah was a new person when she came out of the water of baptism. She had no well-spelt-out theology of this important sacrament that is such a vital marker of Christian identity. She just did it because the Lord said to do it. Yet as she dried herself with a towel she became aware that something significant had happened to her. She began to see and hear everything! Ever since her experience at the hospital, she had seen and heard selectively. It was as if she had been covered by a transparent seal, which she understood to be God somehow protecting her.

Several weeks later, Francinah was introduced to an Apostolic Faith Mission (AFM) church pastored by Rev. Mtsweni. The AFM is a Pentecostal denomination that traces its roots to the Azusa Street revivals at the beginning of the twentieth century. It retains its Pentecostal flavour to this day. Francinah felt more at home with the style of worship and ministry at this church than she did at the Alliance church.

Soon after she started attending the AFM in Mabopane, there was a time of testimonies when believers were encouraged to share their stories. Francinah stood up and told her story, from beginning to the end. The congregation loved it and saw it as the triumph of the gospel of Jesus Christ over the powers of traditional religion. A sangoma turning to Christ is not a usual testimony to come by. After the service Pastor Mtsweni called her aside.

"I loved your testimony very much. You are really blessed of the Lord. But I want you to listen to me carefully," he said. "You are welcome here in the Apostolic Faith Mission. Enjoy our fellowship. Do what we do. You will grow in your faith. But I counsel you not to take membership in the AFM. You are called to be an itinerant preacher, and at this point, the AFM does not embrace women preachers. God will show you how and where you will be able to serve him freely."

Francinah was saddened by these words, which to a young believer felt like a rejection. Later, however, she came to understand the wisdom and strategic value of Pastor Mtsweni's counsel. The idea of women in ministry is still disputed in many churches, and the battle of the sexes can become quite vicious, as Francinah's later experiences were to show.

She continued to hold down her job at the municipality, travelling by train to and from work. Sometimes she was expected to work on Sundays, which left her feeling sad because she did not want to miss the services at Pastor Mtsweni's church.

Victory Tabernacle

A year later, while she was still working for the municipality, Francinah had a run-in with Joseph, her ex-boyfriend. He said some hurtful words to her, which led her to breaking down in the lady's room of the caravan park where she worked. Her colleague Elizabeth, who worked with her as a cleaner, heard her crying and tried to comfort her in her distress.

The distraught Francinah shared about her painful exchange with Joseph and how he was accusing her of using the story of her heavenly vision as a trick to get him to marry her. Unnoticed by the two friends who were in deep conversation, a Mrs Ina Labuschagne, an Afrikaner woman who happened to be in an adjacent bathroom, overheard them.

Ina is a devout woman with a prophetic ministry. She had come to the caravan park on an assignment from God, who told her, "You will find someone there who you must encourage for me." Because she is a white person, Ina naturally assumed the person God wanted her to help would also be a white person, since white and black were separated by the high, invisible wall of apartheid. They had virtually no social or even spiritual relationships or fellowship. But as Ina heard Francinah's anguished sobbing, she knew that this was the person to whom God had sent her.

The caravan park was a place where white people could live in caravans while they holidayed in the area or had a house renovated. Ina had been living there for three weeks and had begun to despair of finding the person she was looking for. Soon she would have to leave the park to go back to her home.

Ina started to ask Francinah about her testimony and was convinced that she had found the person to whom she had been sent. She immediately started to encourage Francinah and disciple her in the faith. Over the next several days, they met every day. Ina gave Francinah a Bible and some Christian books and had daily Bible studies with her.

"Where do you go to church?" Ina asked after a few days.

"I go to the Apostolic Faith Mission church in the township," Francinah replied.

"Apostolic Faith Mission?" asked an obviously concerned Ina.

"Yes, I go to the Apostolic Faith Mission church."

"Don't get me wrong; the AFM is a good church. But it is not for you."

"Eish. Which one is my church then?" enquired a bewildered Francinah.

"Let me go and pray. God will show you which church he wants you in."

Three days later, the two women met again for their Bible study.

"I prayed about the church God wants you to go to, but God said he will not repeat himself. He has already told you which church you belong in. You know the church," Ina said.

Francinah remembered that for several weeks now, every Sunday when she went past the four-way stop at the corner along the route to the AFM church, she would hear a voice deep inside asking, "Francinah, where are you going?"

"I am going to church," she would answer the inner voice.

"Your church is the one you are passing," the inner voice would insist. Francinah had never been to that church. Its name was Victory Fellowship. She did not even know the people there, yet she disliked it intensely. There was no way she was going to that church!

"Ok. You go first," she said to Ina. "You tell me which church it is, and if it is the one God told me about, I will let you know."

"The church is Victory Fellowship, Pastor Victor Mokgotlwa's church in Soshanguve. Do you know it?"

"Eish! Yes I know it, and every time I pass that church, an inner voice tells me that it is my church."

"So why don't you go there?" asked Ina, surprised that Francinah had not obeyed what was clearly God's leading.

"I don't like it. In fact, I hate it!"

"Have you ever gone there?"

"No. I have never set foot there."

Ina concluded that this must have been Satan's scheme to prevent Francinah from going to the spiritual home God intended for her.

Ina belonged to Hatfield Christian Church, a large church on the east side of Pretoria. The church was the organizing centre of many charismatic churches that were often independent church plants. Victor Mokgotlwa's Victory Fellowship was among those churches. This was why Ina knew him as one of the black pastors who was part of the charismatic churches network that regularly met at the Hatfield Church, under the leadership of Pastor Ed Roebert. Pastor Roebert, a former Baptist pastor turned charismatic, was considered by many to be the father of the charismatic Christian movement in South Africa. Ina offered to speak to Pastor Victor the following day at the monthly pastors meeting.

A few days later, Francinah stopped at Pastor Victor's home after work, because it was on her way home. She was warmly welcomed by Pastor Victor and his wife, who also encouraged her to consider attending the Tshwane Bible School nearby. The school was supported by the church and would be good preparation for the ministry the Lord had called Francinah to.

As it was getting dark, Pastor Victor offered to drive Francinah home, where he met her children and prayed with them, promising to see them in church on Sunday.

That night, Francinah had a dream. She saw a hand holding a picture of Pastor Victor Mokgotlwa. Bringing the picture close to her face, a voice asked, "Who is this man?"

Francinah answered, "It is Victor."

The hand slid past, moving from the right to left in front of her face. It came back a second time. "Who is this man?" the voice asked.

"It is Victor," Francinah answered. The hand slid past from right to left.

It came again a third time. "I say, who is this man?" the voice asked as if demanding a deeper response than she had given on the first two occasions.

"The man is Pastor Victor Mokgotlwa."

"That is right. You see this man? He is the one with whom I am pleased. Follow him."

Francinah awoke with a very deep sense of peace about the church. She knew that this would be her new spiritual home, and that her dream was confirmation from above. She remembered the words of Pastor Mtsweni when he said, "Do not take membership in the AFM. Just fellowship with us. One day God will show you which church you must belong to." That day had come.

Train Ministry

Train ministry has become a regular feature in commuter trains in South Africa as preachers take turns preaching the gospel. Francinah commuted to and from work by train, and she seized the opportunity to preach the gospel to fellow commuters. Without any formal training, she would just call people to turn away from their sins, escape the coming judgment, and accept Jesus as their Lord and Saviour. She would intersperse this preaching with her testimony, especially whenever the commuters started to be rowdy and not pay attention to the sermon. Her story never failed to grab their attention. Many responded to the call and became devoted followers of Christ.

One morning as she was preaching, Francinah heard the Lord's voice: "I want you to stop preaching and go home to your mother's house to destroy the remaining altars (magandelo) that you erected to the idols of African traditional religion. They must be destroyed today."

Francinah changed course immediately. Instead of going home to Mabopane, she took a taxi to Ga-Rankuwa, arriving unannounced at her mother's house. It was evening when she got there.

"What brings you here at this time of day, my daughter? Is there a problem?" her mother asked.

"No Mama, God said I must come here," Francinah replied.

"God said you must come here? What for?"

"To destroy my magandelo."

"Iyooo, iyoo, iyoo! I thought I have endured too much from you and your new religion already, but this is way too much! My daughter, that is not done! You will die."

"No Mama, I am going to dig out the gandelo and burn it. Do not worry; nothing will happen to me," Francinah assured her.

Agnes knew her daughter well enough to know that nothing would stop her from following her convictions. Agnes despaired for her. She knew that you never uproot a gandelo, even when you move house. If you want to move it to your next home, you must slaughter a cow, brew some African beer, and call another sangoma to announce to the ancestors that you are moving them to a new dwelling place. To ignore this spiritual protocol is a serious offence to the gods and may result in death. So Agnes resigned herself to watching disaster befall her daughter. She called her children to be witnesses to this folly against the gods, and Francinah called her children, who stayed with Agnes on weekdays, to be by her side.

"If I die, let me die with my children," was Francinah's reasoning. So it was one mother with her children and her convictions on one side and another mother with her children and her convictions on the other side. It was time for a showdown to decide the fate of the gandelo.

Francinah planned to destroy the gandelo with a pickaxe. But as she approached, even before she struck a single blow, everything went pitch black! She was struck by deep darkness and couldn't see a thing. She started to shiver. Only a few month's old in the faith, she was at a loss as to what to do now.

She prayed inwardly, "Lord, you said I must destroy the gandelo. What do I do now?"

The Lord guided her to go some a distance away from the gandelo and pray. An inner voice told her: "When you go back to the gandelo, do not use the pickaxe. Call upon the power of the blood of Jesus, and then use your hands to pull out the reeds from within the encirclement of the gandelo."

These were special reeds cut from specific trees called *ditlhare tsa badimo* – the trees of the ancestors. The reeds represented the different spirits that Francinah had covenanted with.

So Francinah did as she was told, but before she even touched the reeds, they fell on their own. She picked them up and collected the muti and other ingredients within the gandelo. She then used the pickaxe to dig out the rest of the muti that lay buried in the gandelo. All this she put together and burnt.

Then Francinah called her mother: "Mama, here I am with my children. We are still alive! Jesus is Lord."

Agnes was unconvinced. She still felt that the gods were going to catch up with Francinah sooner or later.

"The ancestors will not do any harm to me, Mama," Francinah said. "All seven of them could not even put up a fight against one man at the hospital. How can they do any harm to me now?"

The destruction of the gandelo was the final signal to the spiritual powers of her ancestral religion that Francinah's break with them was permanent and complete. She now belonged to Christ and to him alone.

6

CURRENT MINISTRY

Some who knew Francinah as a sangoma and who benefited from the powers she had were disappointed that she turned her back on the ways of the ancestors and was no longer a sangoma. For them it was a case of a gift wasted and an unnecessary surrender to the Christian religion.

This was the case with one particular woman from the Free State province who used to be troubled by witches. She had been one of Francinah's greatest fans. She had asked her to intervene and do what is called *go theya motse*, loosely translated as fortifying one's house against witchcraft. She had been troubled by a witch for some time and could not sleep at night. Within twenty-four hours of Francinah's intervention, the witch was exposed and left the village, never to return. After that, the woman lived in peace, never troubled by that witch again. When Francinah converted, this woman was so angry that to this day she refuses to speak to her.

Even Francinah's siblings were concerned. As a sangoma, she was an economic asset to the family and had helped them in many ways. Her younger brother Caiphus put it well: "We were shocked and concerned when she told us that she was no longer a sangoma. How were we to live going forward? Who was going to help us financially? What would we eat? But we accepted her choice. She assured us that she was going to help us even more. We were not convinced. But as we watched her progress in the ensuing months, our minds began to change. She extended her small house in Mabopane, making it more spacious and adding more rooms. Even more surprising, she bought a car! This was unheard of in our family. True to her word, she was able to help us more in her new found faith than when she was a sangoma."

Phineas, Francinah's other sibling, was more supportive, even if he did not always understand what she was doing. When she wanted to be a sangoma, he supported her choice, as he did when she later turned to following God and left her employment to dedicate herself to serving in the church. He recalls how, after Francinah's heavenly vision, some people thought she had gone crazy. Being too timid to confront Francinah directly about their questions, they would pour out all their misgivings and questions on him.

"I know my sister," he would say to these curious enquirers. "I may not understand fully what happened to her in her encounter with her God, but she is not mad. She saw what she saw!"

Francinah grew in her faith and accepted the counsel from her pastor Victor Mokgotlwa that she enrol at the Bible school. She became more rooted in the Scriptures. She was a hard-working and focussed student of the Bible. At home, she would often read the Scriptures aloud for herself and her children. As she developed in the knowledge of the Scriptures and prayer, Francinah's spiritual gifts became more and more evident. Encouraged by her pastor, she began to exercise a ministry of deliverance. She helped many sangomas to break free from the bondage of the religion of their ancestors and commit to Jesus Christ as their Lord and Saviour.

"We always used to pray for the deliverance of sangomas and lead them to Christ," said Pastor Victor. "But many of them would relapse and return to their old ways. After sister Francinah joined our church, she was excellent in ministering deliverance to the sangomas and helped to ground them in the faith. Our retention rate of people coming from that background took a dramatic turn upward."

Francinah also grew in the area of praying for the sick, and many report that they received amazing healing after she prayed for them.

Starting the Church

As time went on, Francinah grew in her faith and continued to serve the Lord. She studied the Scriptures and preached the good news everywhere, to anyone who would listen. People soon began to gather around her and go with her as she went about preaching the gospel and sharing her testimony.

Eleven years after her experience at Kalafong Hospital where she committed her life to Christ, Francinah felt called to plant a church. She conferred with her pastor and was released to start a branch of Praise Tabernacle in Section G of the vast township of Soshanguve. This church became the operational base from which Francinah fulfils her divine mission. It is from here that her assignment is supported and nourished. This assignment consists of prayer for self, prayer for others, proclaiming the gospel, and prophetic ministry.

Francinah's devotion to prayer grew. The Lord's word to her was to pray for herself, and then to pray for others in the name of the Lord. She spends extended periods of time in prayer and fasting every year in order to seek the face of God. This practice has laid a strong foundation for her public ministry. Confident in who she is in Christ, Francinah's public ministry is marked by her Spirit-filled authenticity and simplicity, rooted no doubt in her solid prayer and devotional life. These characteristics have made her a much-sought-after conference speaker and evangelist around the townships of South Africa. Francinah's connection with her audiences is immediate and impactful. People feel drawn to her down-to-earth communication and can relate to her township language and idioms.

Francinah's second assignment was to pray for others in the name of the Lord for their deliverance and healing. The first word lays the foundation for the second word. You cannot be a blessing to others unless you yourself are blessed. God's word to the Hebrew patriarch Abraham comes to mind:

> Go from your country, your people and your father's household
> to the land I will show you.
> I will make you into a great nation,
> and I will bless you;
> I will make your name great,
> and you will be a blessing (Genesis 12:1–2).

As it was with the father of faith, Abraham, who after leaving the place and ways of his ancestors first had to receive the blessing from the Lord before he could be a blessing to others, so too with Francinah. After she turned her back on the ways of the world and the ways of her ancestors, she had to learn to appropriate God's blessing in her life through prayer and personal devotion. Then she was ready to be a blessing to others, helping them find healing and deliverance in the name of the Lord.

On the back of the first two assignments, Francinah has become a much-sought-after evangelist and teacher and ministers in the areas of deliverance and prophecy. She travels both nationally and internationally doing ministry among different churches. This ministry is possible because Francinah has trained several pastors who take responsibility for her local church while she is travelling.

The simplicity and unassuming nature of Francinah's ministry and prayer for others stands in sharp contrast with much that happens in contemporary charismatic church life in South Africa. More and more preachers are departing from simply praying for people in the name of Jesus Christ. They use all manner of other articles including water or oil, often sourced from dubious quarters, to perform miracles. While they may be able to point to some or other biblical text to support their use of these things, the real problem is the source of the power they use. South Africa has seen the emergence of numerous preachers who claim to perform miracles while being involved in dark practices. Some put such a spell on their congregants that, at their bidding, the people will do anything. Some have swallowed snakes, eaten grass, and drunk petrol. Other preachers have not been as spectacular but have nonetheless been as deviant from the norm of Scripture.

If these were fringe occurrences at the margins of charismatic Christianity, they would be perhaps easier to ignore. But this obsession with power, signs, and wonders has drawn many pastors in the black townships to do whatever it takes to get power. With power comes the promise of bigger churches as many come to witness the signs and wonders, and the pastor growing increasingly rich.

Francinah's simplicity and biblical faithfulness stand as a rebuke to these tendencies and have endeared her to many.

7

THIS BOOK IN CONTEXT

This book is a labour of love dedicated to a very important story that would otherwise never have been written, because as a general rule, writing books isn't quite what African women from the townships in South Africa do. These women are, in the main, part of an oral culture. They leave the task of writing to other cultures that are that way inclined. A visit to any of the bookshops around the nation's towns and cities will be more than adequate to confirm this claim. The overwhelming majority of the titles on the shelves are by non-Africans.

Francinah's story got my attention because of two broad considerations, one pastoral and the other missiological. I am a pastor by vocation and am concerned about the state of discipleship in the church in South Africa.

A Pastoral Concern

The following example will help shed light on my concern. Several years ago, I took a five-hour trip by car from Johannesburg to Pietermaritzburg with several friends. The Evangelical Alliance of South Africa, which I have the good fortune to serve, was co-hosting a consultation on the gospel and African culture with African Enterprise, which was founded by one of South Africa's finest evangelical leaders, Michael Cassidy.

With us in the car were two rather interesting characters. One was a well-known African traditional religion personality with a PhD in African Traditional Religion (ATR). She was also a practising sangoma with outspoken views on matters relating to ATR, and in particular on

Christians who combine Christianity with traditional religion. Such syncretism, she claimed, was bad for both Christianity and ATR.

The other passenger was archbishop of a large indigenous church with several million members. He believed that Christianity, properly understood and contextualized in his Xhosa culture, has no quarrel with traditional religious ideas like sacrificing to ancestors and interceding through them. We were all friends who had worked together in one context or another in the struggle against apartheid and had the relational capital that made frank conversation possible. There was never a boring moment throughout the long trip as the two had a fascinating duel about African culture and African religion. It was full of humour and rib-cracking laughter!

At the core of their debate was the ATR practitioner's challenge: "You Christians should choose where you belong! Are you with Christ or are you with us and the ancestors? You can't be on both sides. Choose!"

To this the archbishop retorted that she was positing a false and unnecessary choice. God did not require him to be a white man first before he became a Christian. Relating to his ancestors is part of his identity and culture as a Xhosa, not his religion. It is akin to a soccer player accepting Christ as Lord without feeling forced to choose between his faith and his sport. So the archbishop was happy to embrace Christ as redeemer while also affirming his cultural identity. "In fact, in my church, Moss," he said as he turned towards me, "God often reveals to me whom he is calling to be a prophet and whom he is calling to be a sangoma. Both are gifts that God uses to help his people."

The archbishop has a huge following of between eight and ten million people in his denomination, by his estimate. Many other African Indigenous Churches and African theologians make similar claims to those made by the archbishop. The Zion Christian Church (ZCC), for example, is understood by many to be the biggest of the African Indigenous Churches in South Africa. According to one of its members, Simon Moripe, the ZCC is "the vanguard of an indigenous expression of African Christianity. Indeed, this church and other African Indigenous Churches have created a synthesis of African traditional culture and

Christian beliefs. They have formulated a truly African Indigenous Christianity."[1]

To return to our conversation in the car, I must, with all due respect to the archbishop, agree with the ATR practitioner. To combine ATR and Christianity is to compromise the integrity of both. To claim, as the archbishop does, that African ancestors have a mediating role that is cultural but not religious is to deny Africans their legitimate claim to a religion of their own. If ATR is a religion, it must, along with all the religions of the world, decide what it wants to do with Jesus of Nazareth and his claim that "I am the way the truth and the life. No one comes to the Father except through me" (John 14:6).

If the African Indigenous Churches' embrace of ATR is overt and intentional, significant numbers of Christians in other Christian denominations, evangelicals included, are less overt and even mischievously secretive in their flirtations with ATR. As Moripe informs us,

> The African Indigenous Churches are overwhelmed by the members of the western-oriented churches who seek assistance from them with regard to their healing procedure. The fact is that many western-oriented members associate themselves with the African Indigenous Churches and even accept double membership; some even officiate as healers. Admittedly, a large number are reluctant to publicise their involvement with the African Indigenous Churches.[2]

This is very disconcerting, as it suggests that ATR has a wide appeal and influence, even beyond those who are members of African Indigenous Churches.

To be sure, not all African Indigenous Churches and their followers espouse the archbishop's views. There are African Christians who insist, correctly, that Christianity must be appropriately contextualized in Africa. As Byang Kato, the evangelical scholar who spoke years ago at an African conference addressing the same themes, declared to thunderous

---

[1] Simon Moripe, "Indigenous Clergy in the Zion Christian Church", in *The Making of an Indigenous Clergy in Southern Africa*, ed. Philippe Denis (Pietermaritzburg: Cluster Publications, 1995), 107.

[2] Simon Moripe, "Indigenous Clergy", 103.

applause: "Let African Christians be Christian Africans!"[3] Indeed, there is a big difference between the two, and it is possible to be more African than Christian.

Writing in 1975 for *Bibliotheca Sacra,* Kato further elaborated:

> It is God's will that Africans, on accepting Christ as their Saviour, become Christian Africans. Africans who become Christians should therefore remain Africans wherever their culture does not conflict with the Bible. It is the Bible that must judge the culture. Where a conflict results, the cultural element must give way.[4]

So let us be clear. It is important, even necessary, for Africans to encounter and appropriate Christ in their own context. To fail to do so will mean that their expression of the faith, their worship, will be a mere quotation of the expressions of others. It will not be an authentic response of African people to the power of God at work within them. Jesus, it seems, would much rather that those who worship God would worship him in truth and in spirit, or forever remain quiet.

Authentic Christian worship requires a contextualized faith. It is my hope that Francinah's story will be of help to fellow Christ-followers in Africa who are looking to bring the gospel "home" to an Africa alive with spiritual realities.

A Missiological Concern

Francinah's story is also important for its relevance to Christian mission in Africa and beyond.

Before his departure to return to his Father, Jesus enjoined his disciples to be his witnesses everywhere. He had just spent three years teaching them in words and deeds and in signs and wonders about the kingdom of God and the promise of salvation to all people everywhere

---

[3] Paul Bowers, "Byang Kato and Beyond", *Africa Journal of Evangelical Theology* 28, no .1 (2009): 7, http://biblicalstudies.org.uk/pdf/ajet/28-1_003.pdf

[4] "Let African Christians be Christian Africans", http://www.christianitytoday.com/history/2009/june/let-african-christians-be-christian-africans.html

who believe in him. As Jesus was on his way out of this world, the time had come for a global Christian movement to begin. That is the reason he had come.

It is now an established fact that the centre of gravity of global Christianity has shifted away from the West, where it had settled for a considerable length of time after it left its origins in the Middle East almost two thousand years ago. Its vitality and numerical strength is now in the non-Western world. This makes it increasingly important for African Christians to tell their own stories and share their experiences of the old time religion. To remain silent would be to ruin the choral melody of the redemption song Christ intends his church to sing to the world before his second coming.

Then there are considerations that are as pastoral as they are missiological and go beyond the boundaries of the church. After all, to borrow words from John Wesley, "I look upon all the world as my parish; thus far I mean, that, in whatever part of it I am, I judge it meet, right, and my bounden duty to declare unto all that are willing to hear, the glad tidings of salvation."[5]

Put bluntly, the question for post-apartheid South Africa is this, "What will happen if South Africa rejects Christ in its 'body language' if not in its actual words?" The pastoral ministry of the church to the nation requires that no effort be spared to salvage and preserve the Christian heritage that the missionaries of yesteryear bequeathed our nation. The church's missiological imperative demands the expansion of the reign of God in the nation. Not to do so is to invite judgment upon our nation.

The emerging post-liberation environment is increasingly hostile to the Christian faith at several points, but I will limit myself to those issues raised by Francinah's story. These are ATR and the matter of right to life (abortion).

On 27 April 1994, the first non-racial democratic election was held in South Africa. The iconic Nelson Mandela, then aged seventy-two, decided to cast his first ballot at the little known village of Inanda, twenty-four kilometres inland from Durban. This was the home of Rev.

---

[5] John Wesley, "All the World My Parish", Christian Classics Ethereal Library, accessed 5 May 2015, http://www.ccel.org/ccel/wesley/journal.vi.iii.v.html

John Langalibalele Dube, who was elected the first president general of the African National Congress (ANC) at its inception in 1912. Dube, a minister of the gospel and a tireless campaigner for the development of black people, had built a school there named Ohlange Institute. It was there that Mandela cast his first vote. It was an emotional moment not only for this icon of the struggle for freedom, but for the entire black community who had waited for so long to shed their shackles and taste freedom.

Five hundred metres from the Ohlange Institute is Dube's grave. After he cast his vote, Mandela proceeded slowly to where John Dube lies buried. Mandela had to share this profound emotional moment with someone who could understand, someone who, as the first president of the ANC, had started the work that it fell to Mandela to complete. He stood at the graveside in silence, and after some moments of reflection, he started to speak, addressing the departed president: "Mr President, I am here to report that today South Africa is free."

After the elections, the task of rebuilding a new society would begin. In large measure, this task consisted of reimagining freedom and developing a constitutional framework that would codify the ideals of that freedom. Everything understood to be oppressive to the mind, soul and body of African people would be cast aside as a yoke of oppression.

As a Methodist layman, Mandela's graveside conversation with Dube could be taken as merely symbolic, but is an important illustration of the African view of life. Africans believe the dead do not really die; they live on and become the living dead. They have crossed the border between this world and the next and are now numbered among the gods. This is a deeply held conviction that forms part of the African sense of self, and of our religious-cultural worldview. For many, to be truly free therefore requires overthrowing the yoke of colonial religion and returning to the religion of the ancestors, which is the natural habitat of most African people.

Mandela served only one term in office as the nation's president before he gave the reins to his successor, Thabo Mbeki. The latter proclaimed that the time had arrived for an African renaissance, for Africans to be seized with the task of socio-political, economic, and cultural emancipation and renewal.

Mbeki decried what he saw as Afro-pessimism in many non-Africans whose negative assessment of African potential in matters of self-government, economic, social, political, and cultural development posed a stumbling block to the infant nation looking to build itself. His rallying call resonated with many, both in South Africa and across the continent. The idea of an African renaissance was not new, for it had been proposed and ultimately abandoned in earlier years of post-colonial Africa. However, in the Mandela and Mbeki era, a new optimism arose based on the fact that conditions for a credible African renaissance existed in a way they never had before. The idea captured the imagination of the entire continent and was reflected in some of the programmes of the African Union.

Practitioners of ATR saw a golden opportunity and harnessed their chariots to the social, cultural, and political programme of the African renaissance. They gained considerable mileage. Many people understood the political project of the African renaissance to mean the mainstreaming of all things African, including African indigenous religions. With political space created for it alongside other historically promoted and protected religions like Christianity, ATR erupted into a force to be reckoned with in the nation's religious landscape.

Imbued with an air of political correctness after throwing off the yoke of white rule, the more militant adherents of ATR became more aggressive and intolerant towards the Christian faith. Hotel managers were taken to task by ATR activists for allowing Bibles in the rooms of their establishments and ordered to remove them. Christian prayers offered in schools were queried. In some cases, Christian nurses were stopped from praying at health clinics at the beginning of the day. ATR was becoming the new normal, claiming victim status after years of colonial and Christian marginalization.

In a fifty-two-hectares piece of land in Salvokop, just outside the nation's capital, Pretoria, a monument was constructed named Freedom Park. It has become a sacred space in whose precincts African people can reclaim and reassert their religious-cultural roots. In this place, the spirits of those who paid the ultimate price for freedom are invoked and memorialized. This is as close to South Africa's official religion as it is possible to get in light of a constitution that leans towards the secular and considers all religions equally valid.

What does Francinah's story have to do with this?

Francinah cherished her African roots and was raised in every way as a traditional African. She even entered the service of her gods as a sangoma, living with and depending on their powers to help people. Her remarkable encounter with the risen Lord Jesus and her subsequent and dramatic "divorce" from the ancestral spirits suggests at least two matters that merit serious attention by those concerned for African freedom and African redemption.

The Thirst for Freedom

Those who have not endured multi-generational oppression and centuries of racist colonial rule might find it hard to understand the desperate thirst and hunger for freedom. In their long walk to freedom, black South Africans made many friends and borrowed many implements of warfare, including ideological ones. Some of these "friends" insisted that all religions, whether from the West, East, North or South, are "opium for the masses" and have no place in revolutionary practice. Others insisted that religion was irrelevant to public life and ought to be relegated to the private space of inner piety.

Africans endured both of these ideas for the sake of the greater cause of winning the prize of freedom. But deep within, the African thirst for freedom to reclaim their true self remained. They knew that ideology alone could not sustain life. Their thirst for freedom, meaning, and ultimate purpose was far deeper. Put in Christian language, human beings cannot live by bread alone. They desire something deeper and more meaningful. For the African, this translated as the religion of their ancestors. For many people, recovering their humanity required recovering this ancestral religion and rejecting foreign religions.

So when freedom finally arrived, it was like the bursting of a dam. In a sense the Freedom Park project gives expression to this need to reaffirm one's self independently from the colonial narratives of the East and the West. It reclaims the dignity of one's identity and says: "Here, and without apology, is who I am!" Freedom Park is thus a shrine for African spiritual identity, where every year practitioners of ATR proclaim and assert their religion.

But the story of Francinah brings into question the redemptive adequacy of ATR. Put another way, can drinking from the well of ATR quench the thirst endured by the African community throughout the colonial and apartheid period?

Francinah's testimony asserts that the well of ATR is hopelessly polluted by sin and will disappoint those looking to quench their thirst by drinking from it. Rather than quenching our thirst for freedom, that well will lead to a deepening and inescapable bondage to the spirits of the dead.

Delinking Christ from the Colonial Project

One of the regrettable historical facts of Christian presence in South Africa is that Christianity reached the locals in colonial vessels. Therefore, an illusion has been created that Jesus was European. Much Western popular art and theology depicts the Saviour in such terms, losing in the process the Jewish roots of who he was and the context in which the gospel first emerged. As a consequence, upon attaining their freedom Africans are tempted to throw out the bathwater of colonialism and apartheid with the baby of the Christian message.

This point presents a moment of crisis for the destiny of African people: Will they go with the gods of their ancestors or with Jesus of Nazareth? In this valley of decision, there are very few credible witnesses who do not bear the burden of being themselves colonial agents or erstwhile perpetrators or benefactors of apartheid.

Francinah is one such credible witness. She was a devout apostle of the sangoma cult, invested in the ways of the ancestors. Her exposure to Christianity before her conversion was minimal. Her story suggests that African people ought to look elsewhere for a Saviour. Salvation can be found in none other but Jesus of Nazareth who was crucified for the sins of the world, died, and was buried but rose again on the third day and is alive forevermore.

Thankfully, many leading figures in African liberation struggles have avoided the pitfall of looking for redemption in African ancestors. John Langalibalele Dube, whom I have already referred to as the first president of the ANC, had this to say when addressing the 6th General Missionary Conference of South Africa held in Johannesburg in 1925:

> The preaching of the Gospel and the Mission Schools are at present the most truly civilizing influences which work upon the Natives, and upon their influence, more than any other agency, does the progress of the Native race depend. There is no hopeful future for Natives unless the majority of them take hold of the Christian faith.[6]

Francinah was one of those who took hold of the Christian faith, and her testimony is instructive: There is no room for syncretism. Christ alone is Lord. Many African Christians have, as a compromise, tried to hold the Lordship of Christ alongside a belief in their own ancestors as mediators. Presumably in their view, ancestors, alongside Christ, are able to intercede on their behalf to God the Creator of all things.

From the earliest days of the struggles against colonialism and apartheid, Christian prayers were offered in the firm conviction that God would not abandon the people of South Africa to the inhumanity of oppression. Indeed, the early revolt against colonialism was born in African Christian religiosity. What later became our national anthem, "Nkosi sikelel' iAfrica", was a hymn originally composed by Enoch Sontoga, a Xhosa clergyman and a teacher at a Methodist mission school in 1897. The lyrics are a heartfelt Xhosa prayer.

Nkosi sikelel' iAfrika	Lord, bless Africa
Maluphakanyisw' uphondo lwayo	May her spirit rise high up
Yiva imithandazo yethu	Hear thou our prayers
Nkosi Sikelela Nkosi Sikelela	Lord bless us, Lord bless us
Nkosi sikelel' iAfrika	Lord, bless Africa
Maluphakanyisw' uphondo lwayo	May her spirit rise high up
Yizwa imithandazo yethu	Hear thou our prayers
Nkosi Sikelela	Lord bless us
Thina lusapho lwayo	Your family

---

[6] Quoted in R. S. Kumalo, *Pastor and Politician: Essays on the Legacy of J. L. Dube, the First President of the African National Congress* (Dorpspruit, RSA: Cluster Publications, 2012), 196.

Chorus

Yihla moya, yihla moya	Descend, O Spirit
Yihla moya oyingcwele	Descend, O Holy Spirit
Nkosi Sikelela	Lord bless us
Thina lusapho lwayo	Your family

This prayerful hymn became a much cherished song of struggle and comfort in times of deep pain, often sung in the face of police brutality and death as well as at funerals of victims of police killings. It is unthinkable to imagine that the God of justice could hear these heartfelt prayers, offered for over a century in earnestness, tears and deep grief, and remain aloof.

For these reasons a claim can be made that the stirrings and restlessness of the early forebears of the anticolonial struggle were signs that the God of history had begun a good work in the people of South Africa, and that he was determined to complete it. As in the days of Moses, the Lord was the first mover of the Exodus; he was there at the beginning and stayed the course till the end. He remained faithful even in the difficult times when the strength of some failed. For they couldn't endure the long and seemingly unending wait for the promised land and wished to return to Egypt.

It is therefore ironic to witness within a generation the turning away from the God of Enoch Sontoga and other pioneers of the struggle to end unjust rule.

It is my prayer that offering the story of Francinah will contribute in some way to helping those African Christians who are wrestling with the question of how exactly Christ relates to the world of the ancestors. Some do so out of a sense of deep personal anguish, often because they or their loved ones have found themselves called – without much choice – into the service of the ancestors as sangomas. It is my hope that the pages of this book will shed some light on their spiritual pilgrimage and bring their search to an end.

Lastly, I find Luke 4:18–19 immensely arresting and have adopted it as a paradigm in my own ministry. Quoting from the ancient Hebrew prophet Isaiah, Jesus said these words:

"The Spirit of the Lord is on me,
because he has anointed me
to proclaim good news to the poor.
He has sent me to proclaim freedom for the prisoners
and recovery of sight for the blind,
to set the oppressed free,
to proclaim the year of the Lord's favour."

In my years as a pastor, I have come to understand that of all the chains with which the enemy can hold people in bondage, there are none as cruel as spiritual chains. Political and economic bondage are terrible things and can enslave people and rob them of their God-given personhood. But these kinds of bondage can be broken, as any number of liberation struggles that have been waged in the former colonies of European powers have shown. But spiritual bondage is a deeper form of slavery and more difficult to overcome, especially for people who discount the spiritual realm of life. They simply do not have the weapons to mount a credible "liberation struggle" against it. People set free only at the political or economic level are not really free until they are also set free spiritually. Otherwise they are vulnerable to finding themselves captives again, under a new form of oppression and enslavement. Demons, said Jesus, once expelled have a tendency to return with a vengeance that makes the last state worse than the first (Matt 12:43–45).

Jesus understood his mission as being to free the oppressed from their bondage, to release the captives, and to open the eyes of the blind. Often those who are in spiritual bondage are blind to the fact that they are in bondage – they do not see their captivity – which can make their oppression permanent and hopeless.

This book is a testimony to the power of Jesus Christ to deliver those whom the enemy enslaves.

Part of the burden of faithful African Christians is to denounce spiritual slavery and all that adds to, rather than subtracts from, the bondage of African people everywhere.

The Problem of Abortion

Abortion is another matter of concern, another sin, that the epiphany experienced by Francinah highlights. In the euphoria of new nationhood and the task of writing a new constitution and the laws that would govern the new South Africa, the pendulum swung from one extreme to another. If apartheid was a gross denial of human rights, the "solution" was to enshrine human rights to the nth degree. Being the last country in Africa to be free, South Africa went further than most post-colonial countries in building its constitutional framework on the presumably solid rock of the doctrine of human rights. This doctrine, as our policymakers take it, is the shield we need to protect ourselves so that our rights will never again be unfairly infringed upon by another. Laudable as this may be in its intention, the limitations of this ideology as a basis for *national redemption* did not take long to manifest.

Dr Rebecca Hodes, a medical historian at the University of Cape Town who has researched pre- and post-apartheid abortion in South Africa, explains that under apartheid, a woman could qualify for an abortion only if she was judged to be suicidal by two state psychiatrists.

> "That didn't mean that women didn't have abortions during Apartheid," Hodes says. "They did, in their hundreds of thousands. But there was an abortion Apartheid in place, whereby affluent white women could get them from their private gynaecologists."
>
> Or they flew overseas: English-speaking South African women often took short "holidays" to the UK, while Afrikaans-speaking women visited Holland for the same purpose. Black women, who did not have the luxury of such options available to them, would visit "soap injectors", where soap would be syringed into their uterus to initiate an abortion. They would then go to a public health facility. Medical Research Council (MRC) research suggests that in the final years of Apartheid, over 400 black women died during illegal abortions per year.
>
> The year 1996's Choice on Termination of Pregnancy Act marked the passing of one of the most progressive abortion

laws in the world, entitling South African women of whatever age to a free abortion at a public facility.[7]

So it is that a woman's right to choose is seen as fundamental. Whatever the motive or reason for wanting to have an abortion, a woman's human rights, understood in individualistic terms, came to trump family, community, social, and religious rights. The transformation of the system of apartheid came to mean the reversal of its evils without reference to any ethic beyond the ideological.

The consequence of course is that multiplied thousands of abortions are carried out annually, often on girls under the age of eighteen. Young girls can proceed with abortions without the permission of their parents. In the popular imagination, the assumption is often that what is politically and ideologically correct and legal is what is right. Public policy translates to social morality, social norms, and values.

This abandonment of the biblical insight that all life, even the life of the unborn, must be protected has been replaced by the doctrine of pro-choice. The shield of human rights, or more precisely feminist rights, has become the excuse to terminate the lives of hundreds of thousands of unborn children in South Africa since the legalization of abortion.

Mother Teresa, that saintly nun who worked hard to save unwanted children in Calcutta, had this to say about abortion in the USA:

> America needs no words from me to see how your decision in Roe v. Wade has deformed a great nation. The so-called right to abortion has pitted mothers against their children and women against men. It has sown violence and discord at the heart of the most intimate human relationships.
>
> It has aggravated the derogation of the father's role in an increasingly fatherless society.
>
> It has portrayed the greatest of gifts – a child – as a competitor, an intrusion, and an inconvenience. It has nominally accorded

[7] Rebecca Davis, "Abortion in South Africa: A Conspiracy of Silence", *Daily Maverick* (30 September 2013), http://www.dailymaverick.co.za/article/2013-09-30-abortion-in-south-africa-a-conspiracy-of-silence/#.V2rU1zXe3kG

mothers unfettered dominion over the independent lives of their physically dependent sons and daughters.

And, in granting this unconscionable power, it has exposed many women to unjust and selfish demands from their husbands or other sexual partners.

Human rights are not a privilege conferred by government. They are every human being's entitlement by virtue of his humanity. The right to life does not depend, and must not be declared to be contingent, on the pleasure of anyone else, not even a parent or a sovereign.[8]

A case could be made that Mother Teresa, more than anyone in the twentieth century, gave the world a working definition of the word *good*. To say someone is a Mother Teresa is another way of saying that they are good. Her words call us back to the greatness we once knew as people. Our hearts have become cold and hardened with selfishness and self-justification.

I hope this book will be helpful for those seeking God's way in the midst of the ideological deceptions of contemporary society. It is also my prayer that Christians everywhere will pray for the recovery of sight to policymakers who, by their spiritual blindness, condemn millions of children to death through abortion.

Maybe once recovery of sight has been proclaimed to the blind, we will know what it means to be a good society.

---

[8] http://groups.csail.mit.edu/mac/users/rauch/nvp/roe/mothertheresa_roe.html